"Scharen constructively develops a theology of spiritual gift-edness . . . from examples of brilliant musicality in an African American artist and genre that become a trope to examine the transcendent prophetic gifting of voices for racial and social justice. The provocative call to other theologians and scholars is to take seriously the lived experiences of the millennial generation, whose worldviews are cogent for present and future as change agents."

—VALERIE MILES-TRIBBLE, Berkeley School of Theology

"Hip-hop acts have been such an important prophetic voice for the world and for the church, and The Roots have been chief among them. This book effectively uses these hip-hop luminaries as a portal into the larger creative activity of God in hip-hop culture. Scharen is always a clear writer and a sharp historian. I recommend this book to my fellow humans who love hip-hop and love the church."

—DAVID SCHERER, Cofounder of JUSTmove:
Antiracism Education Through the Arts

"With verve, imagination, and White race consciousness, Scharen invites us on an incredible journey into hip-hop. The book is especially meant for those new to the subject but will also win over those who yearn to live out their calling with greater passion, playfulness, and purposeful pursuit of justice. A wonderful example of theology at work in the world."

—BONNIE J. MILLER-McLEMORE, Vanderbilt University,
retired

"*Someone Has to Care* is a deft, thoughtful exploration of the shared tapestry of hip-hop and theological imaginations. Christian Scharen writes with clarity and conviction as both a lover of music and a theologian, reminding us as readers that the play, passion, and purpose of life are serious, joyful matters. The result is a lovely paean not only to The Roots' musical journey, but also to the prophetic possibility within us all."

—KYLE BROOKS, Methodist Theological School

Someone Has to Care

Short Theological Engagements with Popular Music

Series Editor: Christian Scharen

Editorial Committee: Margarita Simon Guillory, Jeff Keuss, Mary McDonough, Myles Werntz, Daniel White Hodge

Short Theological Engagements with Popular Music features theologians who have a passion for particular popular artists and who offer robust theological engagements with the work of that artist—engaging a song, an album, or a whole body of work over a career. Books in the series are accessible, yet deep both in their theological and musical engagement. Each book foregrounds ideas of interest in the musician's work, first, and puts these into conversation with the context and culture, second, and the Christian tradition, third. Each book, therefore, includes analysis of the cultural artifact, cultural context, and the relation to Christian tradition. Each book endeavors, as well, to speak with vitality to the challenges of living with God's mercy and justice in today's world.

Someone Has to Care

THE ROOTS
and Hip-Hop's Prophetic Calling

Christian Scharen

 CASCADE *Books* · Eugene, Oregon

SOMEONE HAS TO CARE
The Roots and Hip-Hop's Prophetic Calling

Short Theological Engagements with Popular Music

Cascade Books
An Imprint of Wipf and Stock Publishers
199 W. 8th Ave., Suite 3
Eugene, OR 97401

www.wipfandstock.com

PAPERBACK ISBN: 978-1-5326-1217-6
HARDCOVER ISBN: 978-1-5326-1219-0
EBOOK ISBN: 978-1-5326-1218-3

Cataloguing-in-Publication data:

Names: Scharen, Christian, author.

Title: Someone has to care : the Roots and hip-hop's prophetic calling / by Christian Scharen.

Description: Eugene, OR: Cascade Books, 2021 | Series: Short Theological Engagements with Popular Music | Includes bibliographical references.

Identifiers: ISBN 978-1-5326-1217-6 (paperback) | ISBN 978-1-5326-1219-0 (hardcover) | ISBN 978-1-5326-1218-3 (ebook)

Subjects: LCSH: Hip-hop—Religious aspects. | Hip-hop—Social aspects—United States. | Roots (Musical group), performer.

Classification: ML3921.8.R36 S33 2021 (print) | ML3921.8.R36 (ebook)

To Rev. Dr. Julius Carroll, and the beloved community at Bethlehem Lutheran, Oakland, and especially to their youth.

Contents

I've had about a thousand pieces written about me. I'd say at least 990 of those were written by white men.

—VIJAY IYER

Acknowledgments

I want here to offer brief thanks to places and people who inspired and supported this project. I offer my gratitude to The Legendary Roots Crew. Without their passionate commitment to the culture and craft of hip-hop, this book would have no subject. I admire and appreciate their musical creativity as well as prodigious talent. I hope the book honors the way they have expressed those ample gifts.

I offer deep and enduring thanks to my pastoral mentor, The Rev. Dr. Julius Carroll and the congregation where we shared a year of ministry together, Bethlehem Lutheran in West Oakland, California. As I explain in the book, the youth introduced me to hip-hop as a way to introduce me to their lives and concerns, and I have continued to learn far beyond the scope of that year. Julius, too, has continued to support and encourage my work over the years, as the generous mentor I knew him to be in our first chapter of work together.

I hold a unique sense of appreciation for the help provided by the website genius.com and the many artists and fans who laboriously check and annotate lyrics to nearly every song imaginable. I turned to this site again and again to check lyrics and learn more about the many clever references, often ones that I might have otherwise missed or misinterpreted.

There are numerous specific places where I worked on the book, and in at least the first case, gave presentations on my in-process work. I gained so much from the space for generative teaching and learning, alongside time to write, offered by Holden Village in the North Cascades, and its then-directors, Chuck + Peg Carlson-Hoffman. Likewise, two stays on the Isle of Man led to chapters 3 and 4. I especially thank the pubs in Peel and Port Erin including The Marine, The Creekside, The Pervil, Two Fellas, The Highwayman, The Central, and The White House. Their excellent "real ales" along with the "full pint law" keep me cheerful and hard at work.

I'm grateful for time with my lovely mother, Victoria, at her Casa Azul in Port Isabel, Texas during the summers of 2019 and 2020. As well, it was a gift to receive the hospitality of my partner's mother, Aida Luz, at her beautiful mountain home in Corozal, Puerto Rico. It was there, at her big live edge wooden dining room table that I finally finished the last chapter and threw my hands in the air in jubilation.

My children Isaiah and Finn are young adults now, and have shared my passion for music since they were little. The album from which this book takes its title, *How I Got Over* (2010) is among their favorites from the Roots.

To Pierrette Comulada who both shares my deep love of music and shared in the last stages of this book, encouraging me to take the time it needed, but also to get the damn thing done, thank you. You are a gift in more ways than I can count, and nothing matters more than simply loving me as I am.

Finally, but in every way the most important, I overflow with thanks to the wild Spirit who blows this way and that, calling me to follow the way of Jesus, listening for how to live my own prophetic voice modeled so powerfully by the Roots.

Notes on Naming Conventions

When referring to the band, I use "the Roots," not "The Roots," although in the press about the band there is lots of variation. I follow the use in Thompson's book, *Mo' Meta Blues,* as it is the way the members of the group name the band.

As for names of artists, it is complicated, since often artists are much better known by stage names than their given names. Tariq Trotter, aka Black Thought, and Ahmir Thompson, aka Questlove, are the most obvious examples, but Michael Archer aka D'Angelo is another. For the Roots themselves, I chose to use a more formal, given last name approach, rather than using stage names or, as they do, first names (Tariq or Ahmir), which feels too familiar for this use. I do this partly out of respect, because I am an interested (white) outsider, not an insider to their group or to the hip-hop culture. However, with other artists who are more tangential to the story, I use both their given and stage names for the sake of clarity, as the average reader might only know the stage name.

1

The Roots of Hip-Hop:
Introduction

Welcome, welcome. I'm delighted to have you join me in this exploration of the Roots of hip-hop. The roots of hip-hop, as in: the Roots—a story of one of the most enduring, multi-talented, and successful groups of the past thirty years in any genre. Yet in order to properly tell their story, I need to also engage the roots of hip-hop, that is, the *story* of hip-hop, a musical culture born in New York's South Bronx during the 1970s. While many different kinds of readers might enjoy taking this journey of exploration, I have in mind first of all people who don't really know either of these stories. If that's you, come along.

I do, however, have something to offer hip-hop fans who already know these first two stories well (that of hip-hop and of the Roots). Alongside the two hip-hop stories I tell here, I also tell the story about what God has to do with the Roots of hip-hop—a theological story, if you will. I describe how, in the process of becoming one of the most creative faith-rooted voices in music today, the Roots' developed a calling as artists. And I do this, in part, to say that you, too, can discover and live your prophetic calling. You can't help but be inspired by the Roots. Yet the best result of that is that you become inspired to be your most playful, passionate, purposeful, prophetic self in the world around you.

While I'll unpack more about my use of the term "prophetic" later, I use the term here intentionally as a way to speak of a core characteristic of hip-hop, and of the Roots, and also, potentially, of ordinary lives like yours and mine. I don't mean to say hip-hop artists, whether the Roots or otherwise, *are* prophets, somehow mirroring the ancient biblical prophets like Moses and Miriam, Deborah or Isaiah. Rather, I mean to say they (and we) might inhabit a prophetic mode, a way of speaking and living that is in line with the witness of the biblical prophets. Howard University Divinity School professor, Kenyatta Gilbert, outlines the characteristics of this mode within the Black Church tradition. The common thread through prophetic speech leads from recognition and naming of systemic injustice to casting a hopeful vision for what just living should be.[1] Much of the music that has emerged from the African American experience in the United States draws on this prophetic impulse. Both the spirituals and the blues, for instance, have at their core a cry at the injustice of oppression. Yet explicitly because the prophetic also envisions how life should be, it also entails visions of beauty and joy. Hip-hop, like the spirituals and blues, has this same "cry" at its root, which is at the same time a longing for freedom.

The Roots embody this prophetic mode, common within hip-hop, and yet they are also a distinctive group within hip-hop, too. Thompson calls them "the last

1. Gilbert, *Pursued Justice*, 7.

hip-hop band, absolutely the last of a dying breed."[2] Given their distinctive place in hip-hop, and in American music generally, the time is ripe for a deeper analysis of their life and work. They are distinctive in hip-hop for longevity, to be sure. Begun by band leaders Ahmir "Questlove" Thompson and Tariq "Black Thought" Trotter in 1987, they have released 13 studio albums along with award-winning collaborations, including the Grammy Award-winning producing credits on *Hamilton: The Original Broadway Cast Recording*. In a fascinating practice meant to show the continuity of their work over time, they have numbered tracks sequentially from 1–17 on their debut album, "Organix" (1993), all the way to 171–181 on their most recent album, " . . . And Then You Shoot Your Cousin" (2014). If this numbering scheme is not hilarious enough, their two compilation albums, *Home Grown! The Beginners Guide to Understanding The Roots, Vol. 1 and 2*, use a negative numberings system, going from track -29 to 0, presuming that these songs prepare listeners to start at the beginning, with track 1 of *Organix*.

Their distinctiveness also comes from their musical virtuosity. In a genre most known for sample-driven songs, the Roots have depended on live musical performance since beginning at Philadelphia's High School for the Creative and Performing Arts. In his pitch for the Roots to be his house band on *Late Night*, Jimmy Fallon said: "You'll be the best band in the history of late night, ever. Because you can play with Tony Bennett, AND you can play with Jay-Z."[3] The band's close association to such neo-soul artists as Michael Eugene "D'Angelo" Archer and Jill Scott, as well as hip-hop artists James Dewitt "J Dilla" Yancy and

2. Thompson, *Mo' Meta Blues*, 4.
3. Mason, "Roots of Questlove's Success."

> In hip-hop, sampling refers to taking a portion (a "sample") of one song and reusing it as the musical basis of another song. The first recorded hip-hop song, 1979's "Rapper's Delight," sampled Chic's hit song of the same year, "Good Times." The website www.whosampledwho.com is one of the best sources.

Lonnie Rashid "Common" Lynn, signal a musical center of gravity, but they display a remarkable stylistic range both on their albums and in the music required as the house band for Jimmy Fallon, now on *The Tonight Show*.

Finally, a deeper analysis of the Roots is called for exactly because of the social credibility of their platform. The house band for *The Tonight Show*, one of the longest-running and most popular shows on television, plays a leading cultural role in American life. To have an African American hip-hop group step into this role signals a cultural "coming of age" for the genre, and a reckoning for a historically white-dominant nation fast moving towards a day when people labeled white will be the minority. I'll return to these themes in the last chapter. In part, this match between *The Tonight Show* and the Roots emerged from Fallon's love of hip-hop. His many variety show "bits" involve numerous hip-hop sketches, including the now multiple-episode "History of Rap" series with Fallon and Justin Timberlake rapping and the Roots performing the music. Playing night after night to an audience of millions along with their extensive social media presence has given them perhaps the most powerful platform any hip-hop group has had to date.

At this point, a savvy reader might ask: Who is leading this journey to better understand the Roots of hip-hop? Bear with me here: if I tell you a bit of my own story, I can make clear where I'm coming from, what some of my commitments are as a music fan, and also as an academic who writes about music. As I share about the Roots, and about my own life, I hope it helps you think about your own life and experience, as well.

In the summer of 2016, as I was beginning the research for this book, I heard the Roots live for the first time. I try to follow this principle: don't write a book about a living artist without seeing them play live. I suppose it is partly about connecting with the real performers, even though they're on stage and I'm out in the audience. I can still feel the connection, sharing a moment together in real time as the band does its show. It is also partly about the communal experience, being in a crowd responding to their music, getting a sense in my body of the kind of people who are drawn to the artists or group.

Admittedly, the Twin Cities summer hip-hop festival, Soundset, highlights many artists so the crowd around me wasn't only there to hear the Roots. Common, a Chicago-based rapper of the Roots' generation, performed just before, and A$AP Rocky, a chart-topping young New York rapper, was closing the evening afterwards. Still, given that four stages were hosting artists simultaneously, and the beer stands were way in the rear, most people standing around me near the main stage were clearly there to hear the Roots. I was definitely on the older end of the crowd, but I fit right in racially: the audience was largely white. I was curious if this would be the case. As in hip-hop generally, the vast majority of the performers at Soundset were black, but the majority of the audience for hip-hop is white.[4] Many aspects of the Roots' live performances are noteworthy, most of which I will save for later discussion. Here, I want to say a bit more about the race question.

Directly addressing the issue of race and hip-hop matters in particular ways when white people—like me, of course—engage hip-hop. Engaging hip-hop means inevitably facing the race question because as Thompson once put it, hip-hop is "a form of upstart black-folk music."[5] Hip-hop was born in struggling neighborhoods in New York City, and many of its leading artists have engaged with the history and current realities of African Americans. This is the case from Grandmaster Flash and the Furious Five's 1982 song "The Message," one of hip hop's earliest records, up to a more recent track, Kendrick Lamar's "Alright," an anthem for the Black Lives Matter movement protesting police brutality. Despite the global dispersion of hip-hop, and the long-standing presence of successful white rappers from The Beastie Boys to Eminem to Macklemore, race in relation to hip-hop remains a fraught question. It is crucial, then, to introduce myself by telling a white story, my story, as a way to explain where I'm coming from as I engage this music. The care I take with the history and culture of hip-hop is especially important for readers who—like me—are learning a history and culture we've not lived, which we are learning from the outside. The music deserves engagement for its own sake, and not simply for my entertainment. Modeling this kind of respectful engagement is a theological issue, and becomes one way for me to be an ally in the fight against racial injustice, so often the subject matter of

4. Bialik, "Is the Conventional Wisdom Correct in Measuring Hip-Hop Audience?"

5. Thompson, "When the People Cheer."

hip-hop.[6] Yet, for those readers who have lived this history and culture, I hope my work is worthy of your reading, too, with credibility shown by my listening and learning carefully, deeply, and with more than a little self-awareness about what I don't—and can't—know.

Over the past few years, feeling despair and anger over the continuing police murders of unarmed Black citizens, I wanted a constructive response on a personal level. I march and protest these injustices but especially after reading Ta-Nehisi Coates's searing book *Between the World and Me*, I desire a personal way to protest my conscription, as he puts it, as part of a "people who believe that they are white."[7] Whiteness as a social construct in the United States context is built upon violence, and especially the enslavement and killing of Black and Native bodies.[8] Part of deconstructing whiteness, I believe, is listening to and learning the history of the United States, including especially how white supremacy was constructed—in law and lifestyle—in the building of the nation. I engaged some of this important history in a previous book about the blues.[9] A way to learn this history is through those genres of music chronicling the struggles and joys of African American peoples. Like the choice to work on the blues, hip-hop made sense for me. I love music, both in the toe-tapping, head-bobbing way of a casual listener enthralled by the beat, and in the total immersion of an obsessed fan analyzing rhymes on Genius.com. But more importantly, my decision to intensively study the history, culture and music of hip-hop made sense because hip-hop

6. Scharen, *Broken Hallelujahs*.

7. Coates, *Between the World and Me*, 7.

8. Dunbar-Ortiz, *Indigenous Peoples' History of the United States*.

9. Scharen, *Broken Hallelujahs*.

is not only a quintessential genre of contemporary global music, but emerged—as did the blues—from the genius of Black culture in the Unites States.

The choice I made to listen deeply to hip-hop also made sense because they told me to do it. The "they" I'm referring to is the group of teens at my Lutheran congregation in West Oakland during my seminary training to be a pastor. As their way of both welcoming and challenging

their new white Vicar (a student pastor), the youth group at Bethlehem Lutheran made a special presentation as I began my year with them: The Fugees, *The Score* and Public Enemy, *Fear of a Black Planet*. They didn't need to say the obvious. I needed to listen and learn if I wanted to be *their* youth pastor. It says something about my racially homogenous upbringing in western Montana that at age 29, this was my introduction to hip-hop. I learned their lesson, and through it, I began my ongoing tutorial in hip-hop culture. I listened to the music, and more importantly, I listened to them tell me about their lives. These two albums point to the whole history and culture of hip hop, and the way it fits lock step with the last forty years (or the last four hundred years) of Black experience in the United States.

But at that time I didn't do the harder work that required, listening beyond these two albums so I could understand the fuller story of the roots of hip-hop. In another sense, then, I didn't *really* take them seriously. Not, that is, until now. While The Fugees and Public Enemy are helpful as entrees into the culture and music of hip-hop, it is difficult to understand the meaning of these two albums without knowing the overall context of hip-hop history and culture. Both albums feature songs about police brutality and distrust of the criminal justice system: Public Enemy's "911 is a Joke" and The Fugees' "The Beast." While these songs, and others like N.W.A.'s "Fuck the Police," have received condemnation from both Republican and Democratic presidential candidates among many others, most in the hip-hop community simply view them as telling it like it is. Chuck D, the MC for Public Enemy, put it concisely: "Rap is Black America's CNN."[10] Such songs show the gap between how white and black people understand life in America, something not overcome without relationships with and listening to Black people, especially from those who "believe themselves to be white."[11]

In fact, in research on social networks, religion scholar Robert P. Jones shows that as recently as 2014, three-quarters of the United States white population had entirely white social networks, and overall social networks of white people were 91 percent white. The consequences of white self-segregation are, for example, a huge disparity in opinions about trusting in the police. In a 2014 PRRI survey that asked people to agree or disagree with the statement,

10. Chang, *Can't Stop, Won't Stop*, 251.
11. Coates, *Between the World and Me*, 7.

"Police officers generally treat blacks and other minorities the same as whites," a majority of white people agreed (52 percent) while less than a quarter of Blacks agreed (23 percent).[12] In the wake of the killings of George Floyd in Minneapolis and Breonna Taylor in Louisville, and the unfolding uprisings through the summer of 2020, opinion shifted and (more) white people are waking up to the long-standing horrors of police brutality and mass incarceration.[13] Whatever your experience, this book is about respectful bridging of that gap, honoring the prophetic voice that is at least one of the callings of the Roots, and of hip-hop in general. Next, I turn from self-introduction to introduce the Roots.

⟿

In a sprawling hour-plus interview at the Red Bull Music Academy, drummer and Roots bandleader Ahmir "Questlove" Thompson was asked about his comment that there was a time when he thought perhaps the Roots wouldn't be successful, and what contributed to the turning point. Thompson's answer is telling. First, he says it could be "low self-esteem talking" but "I always felt like . . . if you know the infamous fable about the tortoise and the hare. Like, the Roots have this tortoise-and-the-hare journey, where a very slow turtle that's running to the finish line, slow and steady, while the rabbit's on the side of the road losing its breath." And then he qualifies the analogy by saying, "We've been running this race for so long that I don't know if there ever is going to be a finishing line." He compares the finish line to what his manager would

12. Jones. "Self-Segregation."

13. Cohn and Quealy, "How Public Opinion has moved on Black Lives Matter."

call a "Bentley moment," in that he always says, "Oh, you and Tariq are just disappointed because you never had a Bentley moment."[14] It is true that the band has never had a run-away smash hit of the sort which would allow an artist to purchase an extravagant item like a Bentley, a made-by-hand British luxury car with a starting price north of two hundred thousand dollars.

The analogy of the tortoise and the hare has been repeated enough times to have a kind of authoritative status in describing the Roots' journey. In part it has to do with what Thompson calls a "kind of working-class, blue-collar" ethos in the band.[15] NPR (and others) call the Roots "the hardest working band in show business."[16] They earn this moniker in part because of the combination of their consistent production of studio albums and tours in support of them, their five-nights-a-week gig as the house band for *Late Night*, and then *The Tonight Show*, multiple collaborations both as musicians and producers, and the various side projects of the band members.

In part, however, the tortoise analogy relates to their honest struggle with critical acclaim matched with moderate sales success. In the hip-hop world, the "hare" experience is more like the Canadian rapper, Drake. His first album in 2010 sold more than half a million copies in the first week, and has gone on to sell nearly two million copies. His album *View*, released in 2016, was critically panned (gaining a Metacritic rating of only 69 out of 100), yet debuted at number one on the Billboard 200 where it remained for an astonishing twelve weeks. Its first week sales were nearly a million, and it is nearing three million over all, the kind of success that put him on Forbes' "Top

14. Thompson, "Questlove (2013)."
15. Thompson, "Questlove (2013)."
16. Moon, "Roots."

Five Richest Rappers" list. Fulfilling the stereotype, Drake does have a Bentley, a White Continental GTC V8, which he featured in the video for his 2012 song, "Started from the Bottom."[17] The Roots' recent albums, while receiving critical acclaim, have tended to sell around 50,000 in the first week after they are released and only one album (1999's *Things Fall Apart*) has ever been certified platinum, a designation signifying one million album sales. Sometimes described as the tension "between the haves and the have-nots," the "tortoise and hare" dynamic in hip-hop has a complicated history at the intersection of artistic freedom and commercial success that I develop more in chapter three below. The Roots represent a particular version of that history, one that begins with Thompson hearing the first hip-hop record, "Rapper's Delight," on Philadelphia's WDAS, FM 105.3.

When "Rapper's Delight" was released commercially in 1980, becoming the first rap record, hip-hop was still primarily a New York phenomenon. Thompson was 11 at the time, at home in his family's snug West Philadelphia brick-row house with his sister. By this age, he was already very musically knowledgeable—his father and mother performed in a popular doo-wop band called Lee Andrews and the Hearts, with whom he began touring early in his life.[18] Yet despite that excellent childhood education in the popular music of the 1950s–1970s, nothing prepared him for hip-hop. He recalls hearing "Rapper's Delight" and "being paralyzed" or being "struck by lightning." Quickly grabbing his tape recorder, he recorded the song and by the next morning had memorized it. "The world," he recalls, "was different forever." But even more so for him: "If

17. Drake, "Started from the Bottom."
18. Gross, "Questlove's Roots."

it was a new birth for music, it was also a new birth for me."[19]

"Rapper's Delight" itself is a bit of a strange story. Understanding where it came from helps make more sense of the "new birth" Thompson describes, both for music and for him. The emergence of hip-hop can't be understood without understanding the post-1960s abandonment of inner-city neighborhoods like the South Bronx, hip-hop's official birthplace. The fires of the late 1960s, sparked by tensions including the assassinations of Malcom X in 1965, followed by Martin Luther King Jr. and Robert Kennedy in 1968, smoldered through the 1970s. In part because the Bronx was a mostly minority, working-class community, New York public works director Robert Moses built the Cross-Bronx Freeway as the first interstate to go through a densely populated urban area, destroying in the process whole neighborhoods and thousands of homes. What had often been diverse, healthy ethnic neighborhoods were razed and large populations of African American and Hispanic citizens were relocated to high-density housing projects under the guise of "urban renewal." The dislocation sent the South Bronx into a tail-spin, losing 600,000 manufacturing jobs over the decade of the 1960s, with average per capita income dropping to $2,400 accompanied by an incredible near eighty percent youth unemployment. Describing this era, hip-hop scholar Jeff Chang writes: "If blues culture had developed under the conditions of oppressive, forced labor, hip-hop culture would arise from the conditions of no work."[20]

In response, businesses left and apartment owners, facing increasingly empty buildings, turned to arson in

19. Thompson, *Mo' Meta Blues*, 24.
20. Chang, *Can't Stop, Won't Stop*, 13.

hopes of collecting insurance. Between 1973 and 1977, 30,000 fires were set in the South Bronx. These were, as Chang puts it, not the fires of rage which burned in the 1960s. Now, "these were the fires of abandonment."[21] The abandonment was not only on the level of mostly white business owners and landlords fleeing to the recently built suburbs of New Jersey and Long Island. A more sinister, official abandonment was also enacted. New York's Democratic Senator Daniel Patrick Moynihan articulated a popular public sentiment among whites—that if the poor minority residents still living in the South Bronx wanted better lives, they would quit burning their neighborhoods down. Behind the scenes, however, he created a more profoundly damaging policy proposal. Chang describes what transpired: "In 1970, [Moynihan] had written an influential memo to President Richard Nixon, citing Rand Corporation data on fires in the South Bronx and bemoaning the rise of radicals like The Black Panthers. 'The time may have come,' he famously wrote, 'when the issue of race could benefit from a period of benign neglect.'"[22] Whatever his intent, and he later complained he was misunderstood, President Nixon penciled, "I agree!" on the memo, serving to justify further withdrawal of education, police, fire, clinics, and other public sector services in poor neighborhoods. The clear message was: enough of this activism for civil rights and racial justice.

While they had never been totally absent, gangs now flourished, controlling territory, and running an underground economy. Flaunting their colors and their strength, each tried to expand their sphere of control either through alliances, or more often, violence. One of the only

21. Chang, *Can't Stop, Won't Stop*, 15.
22. Chang, *Can't Stop, Won't Stop*, 14.

safe spaces for these rival neighborhoods and gang members to meet occurred when DJs set up and played dance parties in halls or outside, at parks or basketball courts. The street reputation of the best DJs—the ones with the best sound system, the largest crowds, and crucially, the most antics, rivaled the gangs for authority and influence.

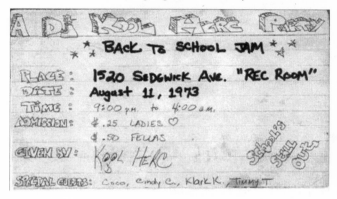

Clive Campbell, known as DJ Kool Herc, was one of the first—and the best. His early parties at 1520 Sedgwick Avenue were modest affairs—mostly bored teens trying to escape the harshness of daily life in a burned-out neighborhood. Born in Jamaica, Campbell's family moved to the South Bronx as a teen. As his DJ work expanded, he and a few friends used the mic to connect with the crowd, imitating the playful rhyming of the Jamaican DJs he remembered from home as a way to set their dances apart. This practice became known in the culture as EmmCeeing or MCing, a kind of host of the dance, working in tandem with the DeeJay to work the crowd.

The five elements of hip-hop include: 1) DeeJaying or DJing: playing the records, and also in early hip-hop, the lead person for an evening dance party; 2) EmmCeeing or MCing: rhyming or rapping to encourage and hype up the dancers, working with the DJ; 3) B-boying/girling: break dancing during the break in the song, usually a percussion section with no vocals; 4) Graffiti writing: artistic representation of the culture usually on subway cars or in public spaces; 5) Knowledge: an embrace of Afrocentric history.

In another effort to make his shows stand out among all the DJs active at the time, Campbell noticed the wild dancing during the instrumental percussion-driven breaks in songs. A pattern had developed where the crowd would step back to create a circle into which excellent dancers would shimmy and flip and spin, showing off their moves. Thanks to these "break dancers" as they began to be called, Campbell started to hone in on songs with longer breaks, like James Brown's live version of "Give it Up or Turn it Loose." He then had the brilliant idea he called the "Merry-Go-Round," working two identical records on adjacent turntables, and as one finished the break, he would have the other cued up for the beginning of the break, thus creating a loop extension of the break.[23]

Many other DJs and MCs were present early on, including perhaps most famously Africa Bambaataa and Grandmaster Flash and the Furious Five. Still, hip-hop culture was a live culture, and took place in community,

23. Chang, *Can't Stop, Won't Stop*, 79.

at and around dance parties. While it is not clear exactly when, the MCs' playful language included the phrase, "hip-hop." As Jeff Chang notes, "the origin of 'hip-hop' goes back to the days when rapping was really about MC-ing, the lost art of moving the crowd."[24] Keith Cowboy, one of Grandmaster Flash's Furious Five (all MCs who worked his DJ events), began to play with rhyming, for example: "I said a hip-hop, a hibbit, hibby-dibby, hip-hip-hop and you don't stop." It was a version of what in jazz is called a "scat" vocal, following the rhythm of the song and the movement of the dancing. And it stuck, becoming widely imitated, enshrined in the first rap record and finally applied—in the title of the first published article about the movement—as the name of what these gifted youth were making. Though long out of print, in the article, author Steven Hager asked Afrika Bambaataa what he called this youth movement, and Bambaataa said, "This is hip and when you feel that music you gotta hop to it, so that's when we called it 'hip-hop.'"[25]

It wasn't long before the street phenomenon of the dances with their flamboyant DJs and MCs came to the attention of record labels. Black indie record label owner Sylvia Robinson, of Sugar Hill Records (Sugar Hill is a neighborhood in Harlem) tried to sign prominent early artists including Grandmaster Flash, but they laughed at the idea, arguing it was an event, not a song, and couldn't be put on a record. Robinson and her son, Joey, found three rhymers (Henry "Big Bank Hank" Jackson, Guy "Master Gee" O'Brian, and Michael "Wonder Mike" Wright, brought them into the studio, and recorded "Rapper's Delight" over a sample from a hot R&B hit by the band

24. Chang, "How Hip-Hop Got Its Name."
25. Hager, "Afrika Bambaataa's Hip-Hop."

Chic called "Good Times." It raised a host of issues, not least of which was authenticity. Rap historian Shea Serrano describes the issue: "The group [was] three guys from New Jersey, as piecemealed together by a woman named Sylvia Robinson . . . who had been exposed to rap almost by accident and decided she wanted to record a rap record."[26] Still, it was a smash hit, becoming a best-selling 12 inch single, and in the process made hip-hop part of popular culture.

Of course, there were thousands of young boys and girls hearing this song, just as Thompson and his sister did that evening on a Philadelphia radio station. Hip-hop had broken out beyond its New York-area birthplace. Yet something else dramatic happened, as well, with this recording. In early live hip-hop, the DJ was the center of the show, the lead name on the billing, with the MCs working with and for the DJ (think Grandmaster Flash and the Furious Five—a DJ and his five rhyming MCs). However, with "Rappers Delight" there was no DJ. All of a sudden, the pattern flipped, and the rhyming skills of the MC became the focus. While some hip-hop groups continued to have a DJ as part of the mix (think: Norman "Terminator X" Rogers of Public Enemy, active into the late 1990s), they now took a back seat to the rappers, launching a new era of the genre.

∽

Thompson and Trotter both were influenced by the new emphasis on MCing and their subsequent partnership as rhythm and rhyme fit the new mold. While their decades-long partnership at the heart of the Roots began

26. Serrano, *Rap Year Book.*

in high school, they couldn't have been a more unlikely pair. As Thompson later put it:

> We were like negative images, each of us seeing something in the other they had never seen before. I saw this kid living on the edge, dabbling in all the dangerous areas of urban life. He saw an awkward black kid with an optimistic outlook, a sheltered Christian devoted to clean living, naive about girls, not really able to participate in thug life at any level. At the same time, I saw his sensitive side and he saw that I had a hidden self-confidence and self-possession.[27]

Neither of them expected to end up at the same school, let alone become friends with one another. But the fact that they did, and that it was a high school for the creative and performing arts, influenced their development, especially the choice to have a live band rather than sample beats from records.

It was no surprise to see Thompson end up at the Philadelphia High School for the Creative and Performing Arts (CAPA). His musical parents saw his gifts early, and he recalls getting his first drum set for Christmas at age three. As he grew, he went with his parents on tour, helping navigate, prep wardrobes, learning to run the lights, how to set the staging. His father tutored him in all the backstage tasks of a touring band, and all before he even hit his teens. Then, before a memorable show at Radio City Music Hall the drummer hurt his arm and his father said, "You know the gig, you play the show."[28] Thus he became the band's touring drummer at age thirteen.

---

27. Thompson, *Mo' Meta Blues*, 75.
28. Ghansah, "Don't Let The Green Grass Fool You."

While the touring gave him an expansive musical knowledge, he was considerably more tied down at home. With devoted Christian parents and grandparents, he spent long days at church on Sunday, and attended a private Christian school during the week. With the 1980s crack epidemic raging on the streets of America's cities, Trotter recalls Thompson's parents "kept gates on windows and a gate on the front door that was locked by a padlock. And if we couldn't find a key to the padlock, we'd just be locked up in the crib. He was never in the streets because they sheltered him from that. His whole life he has been a musician, like his father."[29] He survived a couple of early years at a Christian high school, digging deeply into The Jungle Brothers, De La Soul, and other Native Tongues hip-hop to survive. But after rebelling, and begging to transfer to CAPA, his parents relented.

While they met on the second day of school in an incidental way, Thompson and Trotter didn't really start hanging out until Thompson promised a girl he was sweet on that his group would perform at an upcoming school talent show. With the name Radio Activity, and future world class jazz bassist Christian McBride joining in, they performed publicly for the first time playing a loop from James Brown's "Get on the Good Foot."[30] Soon, they were down on South Street—a trendy neighborhood in downtown Philly—playing for change, joined then by Joshua Abrams on bass. Abrams, who they called "Rubber band," became, like McBride, a very successful composer and professional musician. On the first day, they made $80 and got a huge charge from the audience gathering around them. Over time, they began to get business cards and gig

29. Ghansah, "Don't Let The Green Grass Fool You."
30. Thompson, *Mo' Meta Blues*, 71.

offers in their jar, along with the dollars. Afternoon street gigs turned into evening party gigs.

While it seemed a natural fit for the musical Thompson to end up at CAPA, Trotter's traumatic and difficult childhood makes his arrival at CAPA more unlikely. Born the same year as Thompson, but on the tough south side of Philly, Trotter's parents were part of the "Black Mafia," a Nation of Islam-related organized crime group responsible for drug trafficking (especially heroin) but also robbery, extortion, gambling, and prostitution. His father was killed execution-style when he was only two, and he was sent to live with his maternal grandmother, a strict church-going influence. "Where I'm from, the life expectancy is about 25 or 26. My father was murdered at 26. I remember when I was 15 or 16 years old, I couldn't imagine what life would be like past the age of 30, just because I didn't know that many men who had lived beyond their 20s," Trotter recalls.[31]

The hardship as well as the hope is laid out powerfully as Trotter rhymes an intro to John Legend and the Roots' cover of Donny Hathaway's 1972 hit, "Little Ghetto Boy." "My grandmother suits was tailor made/Sundays Mahalia played," he begins. He recalls her simple ways, her kneeling to pray, and the sternness of the pastor's preaching. Yet his reason for being with her becomes clear: "What my father was into sent him to his early grave/then mom started chasing that base, like Willie Mays." He depicts the drugs and death, and a childhood that was "all of 40 night and 40 days." The biblical illusion to the great flood (Gen 7) allows his unfolding rhymes to evoke water and chaos, creating a sense of drowning, but he names music's saving role: "Music my therapeutic way to cope with all this pain

31. NPR Staff, "Roots Weave a Tale of Crime and Karma."

/ Was headed for the drain, soakin before the rain / water came and chaos, until the order came." He found a way to start again, to escape the chaos, as he puts it, "tryin to move out of the dark, and closer to the light."

It turns out, however, that his mom played an important role in his artistic development. She saw his interest, and sent him to art school on Saturdays, to summer art camp, and the arts became his escapism, a way to get away from "the block." Thompson recalls: "He was one of those thug creatives, a kid who kept up street appearances and projected toughness but who was also immensely gifted as a visual artist. He could draw, paint, sculpt. He could do anything. . . If we hadn't started the Roots together, if he hadn't become a hip-hop star, I wonder what he would have done in the visual arts."[32] But Trotter had been doing rhymes since he was little, and his sharpness was equal to none. In Thompson, he had his partner-in-crime, a veritable walking catalog of beats at his fingertips. It was, as they tell the story, the cool kid and the nerd. "All of a sudden, I have this thug-ass art student who'll only let me sit next to him in the cafeteria if I do break beats for him," Thompson says.[33]

While Thompson and Trotter have been the mainstays of the band, there have always been others. The first members were a rotating group connected to CAPA and their circle of friends in Philly. The Roots' independent debut *Organix* released in 1993 was largely recorded live and included a range of these early collaborators—including bassists Josh "Rubberband" Abrams and Lenard "Hub" Hubbard, MCs Kenyatta "Kid Crumbs" Warren, Malik "B" Basit-Smart, and Karl "Dice Raw" Jenkins, beat-boxers

32. Thompson, *Mo' Meta Blues*, 54.
33. Bilger, "Rhythm in Everything."

Rahzel Brown and Kyle "Scratch'" Jones, as well as early keyboardist Scott Storch. Their current crew, save bassist Mark Kelley who joined in 2012 after Owen Biddle left, has been the same for a decade. In addition to Thompson on drums and Trotter with MC duties (in the center of the photo), the members include (left to right) James Poyser on keyboards, "Captain" Kirk Douglas on guitar, Frank "Knuckles" Walker on percussion (dropped from the lineup in 2017), Damon "Tuba Gooding Jr." Bryson on sousaphone, Kamal Gray on keyboards, and Mark Kelly on bass. For the *Tonight Show* band, David Guy and Ian Hendrickson-Smith, horn players for Sharon Jones and the Dap-Kings, regularly join in.

My developmental story of the Roots frames the book's theological argument. In Christian theology, God is seen as the creator of all things, the force of love who holds everything in its being. And human beings are endowed with spiritual gifts that allow them to be in relationship to God, to one another, and to the creation. We are, as the biblical creation story puts it, given the task to "tend and keep" the world (Gen 2:15). In doing this work of tending and keeping, people make use of many different gifts, gifts given by God's Spirit to each person. Christians believe this spiritual giftedness to be confirmed in baptism, and to grow or develop across one's lifetime. In Saint Paul's first letter to the church in Corinth (chapter 12) he develops the position that while there are clearly a variety of gifts, it is the same God who activates them all. However, to clarify their end or purpose, he notes that each is given a manifestation of the Spirit, expressed as a gift or talent, to be used for the common good and not for one's individual benefit alone. To underline this point, he uses the metaphor of the body. While there is one body, there are many parts. While they are all different, nonetheless they are all essential to the functioning of the whole. And in reference to the Bible's consistent ethic of concern for the most marginalized, Paul argues the good of spiritual gifts ought to be in service of those in need, that is, spiritual gifts are given with a preferential option for those who are suffering.

This developmental theory of spiritual gifts is sometimes described in terms of the journey of finding a "calling" or a "vocation."[34] By this, I don't mean simply finding a job. It is something deeper, something about how the distinctive gifts one has, and that are nurtured by both family and community, find their way out into the world to meet its needs in one way or another. Tony Wagner, an education professor at Harvard, has developed a simple framework for this developmental journey. He describes a period of play in which a context is set for exploring—and finding—one's gifts. The first period of play opens into a

34. Cahalan and Miller-McLemore, *Calling All Years Good.*

second period marked by passion, digging into those areas that, in children's play, they discover themselves to be both very good at, and often for that very reason, to find deeply joyful, too. While exploring a passion, people often begin to see how the world might need such gifts, and a third period unfolds in which this paring between one's gifts and the world's deep need become clear, offering a sense of purpose in the world. It leads to an existential center, a kind of grounding self-knowledge about what one is good at, and a kind of satisfaction that that thing is needed, that it is of service to others.[35]

Play, passion, purpose; this frame helps, I think, to show the unfolding development of the Roots, and their particular mode of playful, prophetic hip-hop now enjoying one of the most prominent platforms one could hope for on *The Tonight Show*. It may also help all of us to discern a pattern to our unfolding journey in finding our prophetic callings, and their purpose in the world. To the first step of that journey, play, we now turn.

35. Wagner, *Creating Innovators*, 27.

2

"Good Music": Playing for Fun

Against a backdrop of a graffiti artist working his genius on a South Philadelphia brick wall, two men rhyme: "One to make you scream, two to make you shout, three for the Roots, turn it out, turn it out." A young Ahmir Thompson begins beatboxing, a form of vocal percussion serving as the rhythm underneath his partner, Tariq Trotter, who launches into an extended freestyle rap. Midway through the three-and-a-half-minute flow of rhyming, Thompson wanders over to the wall, beckons Trotter, and starts pointing to, and calling out, colors. "Blue," Thompson says, almost as a taunt. Trotter, on beat, picks it up: "Blue, blue, who the hell are you, I am the one that's from the Root's crew, and I'm telling you, to rebel!" The scene, shot for a 1990s hip-hop graffiti video magazine feature, shows the playful nature of hip-hop, and of these young, talented artists. The graffiti artist, Stephen Powers, who was both editor of the magazine and a famous graffiti artist in his own right, known on the streets by his tag "ESPO," is busy throughout, but only at the end of the video does the viewer see what he was writing on the wall: "The Roots."[1]

Noting that some people point to this video on You-Tube as early proof of Trotter's MCing talent, Thompson laughs and says, "I don't need that as proof: I go right back to CAPA in 1988, watching Tariq dismantle kids at the lunch table" to the point they would want to fight him. Rap has always had that competitive aspect, a sort of alternative mode of fighting, and Trotter's love of the battle drew him to Thompson, his go-to guy for beats. As unlikely as their "nerd meets cool kid" relationship was, Thompson's mastery of early sample machines like the Casio SK-1 he got for Christmas one year made him indispensable as a sideman. While still a drummer, he got excited by the prospects of producing new sounds out of old.

Thompson's adult description of his childhood (and life-long) fascination with sampling technology displays his playful brilliance. Drawing on the literary scholar, Roland Barthes, Thompson describes the principle:

1. Powers, "Roots Freestyle Video," and Schwartz, "Street Art and Subversion from Stephen (ESPO) Powers."

> A text is not a unified thing, but a fragmentary
> or divisible thing, and that the reader is the one
> who divides it up, arbitrarily. Reading is one act
> that creates the pieces. . . With the SK-1 you, as
> the listener, pick a piece of sound, a snippet of
> speech, or a drumbeat, and you separate that
> from everything around it. That's now a brick
> that you have in your hand, and you use it to
> build a new wall. It also lets you take things that
> were transparent, that were previously thought
> of as words and sounds that you look through
> to see other words, and make them opaque. You
> can take the invisible and make them visible.

This perspective fits Thompson's experience that when listening to music he is "drawn into the more experimental material." His parents noticed, as well. As a child, they were struck that he "never focused on the obvious melody or the lead singer."[2] The SK-1 allowed Thompson's playful, creative focus on the backbeats to pair with Trotter's wordplay. These mutually playful, creative abilities in the end made them necessary for each other, and helped to cement their curious friendship.

God and Play

Play, then, is the first stop on the journey exploring the Roots of hip-hop. Tony Wagner unpacks how play works as part of finding one's purpose, one's way to, as he puts it, "change the world." Play, it turns out, flourishes with supportive structures around it. Human beings are born, he says, with an innate desire to experiment and explore in the world around them. Not all contexts—families, schools, neighborhoods—foster this freedom. Yet when

2. Thompson, *Mo' Meta Blues*, 67–68.

its impact is most profound, supportive structures for play allow children the freedom to safely explore the world. It is no coincidence, Wagner writes, that leaders of todays most innovative organizations—Google, Amazon, Wikipedia—all attended Montessori schools. Founded by Maria Montessori, these schools are centered on the role of play in human learning.

In fact, play not only is fundamental to human learning, but constitutes a crucial feature of being human. In his major book *Religion in Human Evolution,* sociologist Robert Bellah argues that play has a fundamental role in the evolution of human culture and religion, including the rise of prophetic religion during the so-called "Axial age" when most of the world's great religions arose. Drawing from studies of play in mammals and early human cultures, Bellah argues play offers us "offline" time, outside of the work of providing the necessities of life. It often, because of this, includes "an element of sheer joy."[3] As play took on ritual dimensions in culture, it offered "the serious possibility of saying, 'Look, the world the way it is didn't have to be that way. It could be different.'"[4] This realization is at the heart of the emergence of the blues in Mississippi delta juke joints feeling the freedom of love and heartbreak in songs like "Love in Vain," or in churches where the swell of the spirituals could uplift parishioners with visions of "How I Got Over." In West African cultures, as in many cultures worldwide, the playing of music, with its rhythm and instrument and voice, created a space for the spirit, and, as Thompson puts it, "blues and gospel were fraternal twins" in this regard.[5]

3. Bellah, *Religion in Human Evolution,* xxii.

4. Bellah and Horn, "Where Does Religion Come From?"

5. Thompson, *Mo' Meta Blues,* 10. Also see Cone, *Spirituals and The Blues.*

In biblical terms, the thread of play might be seen as a thread of the Spirit, the same one who "hovered over the waters" at the creation (Gen 1:2) and who descended upon the prophets of Israel, allowing them to speak a word from the Lord, and not just from themselves (Isa 61:1). It was this creative spirit, able to see how the world could be different, that Jesus drew upon in his first sermon (based upon a reading from the prophet Isaiah), proclaiming "good news to the poor" (Luke 4). The radical freedom of this playful, creative Spirit who resides with Jesus is made clear in a number of key passages. John's Gospel describes how followers of Jesus must be "born of the Spirit," who is like the wind. It "blows wherever it pleases" (John 3:8). This freedom was exemplified in Jesus' compassion for those who were outcasts and sinners. He shocked his contemporaries in saying "I came not for the righteous, but sinners" (Mark 2:17). In fact, Jesus uses music as the measure of his critics, saying in effect, they did not play with him! "We played the flute for you, and you did not dance; we sang a dirge, and you did not weep" (Matt 11:17).

In a sense, the witness of Scripture is pointing to God's wildness, and deep desire to play with creation as a means to seeing what it is to be fully alive. Irish poet and theologian John O'Donohue speaks of the Spirit as the "breathing" of the Holy Trinity, its "spiratio." "This ancient recognition," he writes, "links the wild creativity of the Spirit with the breath of the soul in the human person."[6] It is this connection to breath that brings inspiration, itself derived from the same Latin root for breath. In a similar way, theologian Courtney Goto defines "revelatory experiencing" as a way to name the open-ended and creative process of invitation and participation as a community in

6. O'Donohue, *Anam Cara*, 69.

30

the life of the Spirit.[7] The primary goal in such "revelatory experiencing" is that the Spirit changes us and the world, in the process bringing about a "more just and peaceful world."[8] It is not the same as God's actions with and for us, but, more particularly, our "human role in preparing for, receiving, and participating in the processes of the Spirit."

While the theology of play is an underdeveloped theological category, several of its characteristics I've explored above help illumine the Roots. It is, first of all, an openness, an exploration of possibility. Play is not the territory of law but the playground of grace, of freedom, as Goto puts it. Then, second, play is an expansion of the human soul, and is in that sense a participation in the work of God's creation. This is what the early church theologian Ireanaus meant when he said, "The glory of God is a person fully alive." Play is also, following from that sense of expansive aliveness, a space of our full emotional capacity, expressing sorrow and pain of hardship and suffering, as well as deep joy and hope for the abundant life God desires for the whole creation. And play, fourthly, is a space for growth and learning, as Goto describes. Play, lastly, is not an isolated reality but a communal, relational reality. God is, as Trinity, interpersonal and relational, and in participating in the life of God by the power of the Spirit, we find ourselves drawn into play with "all things" (John 1:3).

Openness, fullness, being alive, learning what is and can be, and in the company of others; this is the territory I mean when I evoke play. No wonder Tony Wagner points to Montessori education, a model for learning that is about structuring just such a playful learning space. As I now turn to explore the early work of the Roots, these themes

7. Goto, *Grace of Playing*, 4.
8. Goto, *Grace of Playing*, 4.

will help illuminate the ways they began their particular playful musical journey as a band.

The Roots at Play

Early on, both Thompson and Trotter had encouragement and space to play with their preferred art forms, including percussion and rhyming. From their bedrooms to the lunch room at school to a Valentine's Day talent show, their playing led them to explore and find a space for a shared creative outlet. But then Thompson graduated from high school. In order to keep Trotter out of trouble, his grandmother sent him to live with relatives in Detroit. It seemed as if the budding collaboration was at an end just as it began. As fate would have it, however, before the year was out, an incident in Detroit led to Trotter coming back to Philadelphia, and the duo were reunited.

Inspiration sometimes comes sideways, from an unexpected source, and so it was that these friends took the next step in their musical exploration. On the train back from New York where Thompson was attending a scholarship audition for the New School for Music, a girl mistook Thompson for a musician named Chocolate (Larry Wright) featured in a Spike Lee-directed advertisement for Levi's jeans.[9] In the commercial, Chocolate is drumming on buckets on the street corner, and he did actually look quite a bit like Thompson! As it turns out, the next day, as they were watching *Soul Train*, the ad came on, and Trotter excitedly said, "Hey, why don't we just do it?"[10] That very day they were on South Street, doing bucket break beats with spontaneous lyrics, and a large crowd gathered. After

9. https://www.youtube.com/watch?v=ZKb7i4JDfKs.
10. Thompson, *Mo' Meta Blues*, 76.

recounting the thrill of the experience to a friend from school, bass player Josh "Rubber Band" Abrams, he asked to join them. The next week they were a trio.

As they played week by week, regulars began to hang out, and some of them, rapping friends of Trotter's, would join in. If you know anything about Thompson, it is that he is a musical encyclopedia, and as such, his musical influences are very wide. Yet both he and Trotter had grown up under the sway of a group of second wave hip-hop groups from the New York area who banded together in a loose collective called the Native Tongues.[11] Comprised of a trio of Afrocentric hip-hop groups—Jungle Brothers, A Tribe Called Quest, and De La Soul—they were influenced by and carried on the spirit of the father of Afrocentric hip-hop, Afrika Bambaataa and the Zulu Nation. Their socially conscious lyricism and jazz-influenced sound created some of the most influential albums of the past half-century, and deeply influenced the style of the Roots.

In a sense, this "collective" idea has been a key influence on the shape of the Roots from their early days on the streets of Philadelphia where they had taken on the self-professed "nerdy" name, the Square Roots. With Thompson and Trotter as the steady center, the Roots have included a flowing and very large group of collaborators engaged with the band, starting with MC Kenyatta "Kid Crumb" Warren who began jumping in with them on the streets and contributed to their first self-produced album, *Organix*. After meeting their soon-to-be manager, Richard Nichols after an impressive performance at a talent show, they recorded two early songs, hoping to develop an album to help launch the group: "Anti-Circle" and "Pass the Popcorn." What struck both Nichols and his friend,

11. Thompson, *Mo' Meta Blues*, 78.

Joe Simmons (aka AJ Shine) was the end of "Anti-Circle." When Trotter spits the line, "So yo this trick is for tha rabbit/I grab it and snatch it inspect it like gadget," a play on the popular television show Inspector Gadget, at that exact point the beat drops out and Abrams takes out his bow and plays the Inspector Gadget theme song on his bass. It is a beautiful example of how they play around, having fun, and connect with their audiences in ways that bring smiles (and offers for recording contracts, apparently, as well).

But when Trotter's friend and fellow rapper, "Malik B" Abdul-Basit volunteered the emerging band for a jazz hip-hop festival in Germany, the occasion finally forced the recording of their first album. That process, in turn, brought together the next, larger iteration of the group. After the summer on the street corner, Abrams went off to college (and, it turns out, a very distinguished career as a composer, bassist, and improviser).[12] Kenyatta Warren left as well. They added Malik B as a second rapper, invited a very talented bassist, Leonard Hubbard, and added a new element, Scott Storch, on keyboard. Nichols, their new manager, felt they should get an album done to sell during the gigs in Germany. It was this group of five who went into a studio and over four days recorded the additional songs for *Organix* (1993), basically including everything they'd played on street corners the previous summer. Many of the tracks have a very playful live feeling, and one, track 10 titled "Essawhamah? (Live At The Soulshack)," was indeed recorded live.

12. https://joshuaabramsmusic.com

Track 6, "Good Music," is a great example of play-fulness, a song that begins with a slow and easy bass and piano groove, with Thompson intoning, "Peace to all the hip cats, all the nappy sweets/This is the brother Question broadcasting live" with "good music" so the audience can "sit back, relax, and dig the groove." Trotter's rhymes playfully narrate their travels with "Rubber Band and Bes." The bass player, Abrams, nicknamed "Rubber Band," had an old car named "Bes." But Bes broke down, with the re-sult that "The Roots is out, to the subway." The hook is, in this era of the band, almost a mission statement: "Does anybody like real music? (yeah!) Sweet music, soul music? (yeah!) You know, the Roots is a group that'll choose it, (what?) Just to use it, (what?) to make you move it (yeah!)" The song—and the album as a whole—embodies this spirit of musical and lyrical playfulness, including The Ses-sion, a 12:43 track with no less than six MCs, including for the first time a female MC, Shortie No Mas (Theresa Thompson—no relation to Ahmir Thompson), and the final two cuts that are literally just brief instrumental jam sessions. Its strengths are also its weaknesses, a wandering, unfocused feel that comes from the exploratory period of play this album represents.

Their second album, *Do You Want More??!!!?!* (*DYWM*, 1995), was similarly loose and playful, released just over a year later as their major label debut (DGC Records, part of Geffen). Under pressure to get an album ready, Nichols told them they had to "pull another *Organix*," meaning he basically locked them in a studio for four days, and at the end, they had an album. This fact alone accounts for the similarity between the two albums, but while *Organix* didn't produce songs with longevity in their live sets, that is not the case with *DYWM*. Tracks such as 19, "Proceed," 21, "Mellow My Man," and 29, "Swept Away," not to mention the one song repeated from *Organix*, "Essaywhuman?III?!," continue to show up in live sets. In the wisdom of decades of perspective, critics see it as one of the classic albums of jazz rap. Yet at the time, it felt like playful, improvisational, and jazz-oriented style was too out of the mainstream to be marketable.

A friend named Gilles Peterson at Mercury, another label that courted the Roots, talked them into releasing an EP with 8 of the 16 songs under the title *From the Ground Up*, an accompaniment to their impending tour in the UK and Europe. Yet the tour itself was a bomb, and the band came back to the US totally broke. After their return, Geffen released the first single from the album, track 20, "Distortion to Static," and it was a bomb, too. They decided to go on a road trip to promote the album before it was released, but that, too, was discouraging. Nonetheless, in advance of the album dropping, the label threw a big party, and the band played a beautiful version of "Essaywhuman?!!!??!" that ended up on the album. And as the album came out, the group toured hard anyway, trusting the advice from their label that they should take the long view. By their fourth album things would be different.

Still, the album marks some stunning moments in their playful discovery of their talents and those of their growing community of friends. Take "Essaywhuman?!!!??!" (track 28), for example, that has saxophone luminary Steve Coleman playing. The album as a whole includes a group of outstanding avant-garde jazz musicians including Coleman, Joshua Roseman, Graham Haynes, and Cassandra Wilson. All of these musicians had been part of Coleman's M-Bass Collective, which he founded about a decade earlier. M-Base stands for "Macro-Basic Array of Structured Extemporizations" meaning, for them, a way of "expressing our experiences through music that uses improvisation and structure as two of its main ingredients." It is not a musical style, but rather a concept, a philosophical approach to creativity in music, "based primarily on music from Afrika and creative music of the Afrikan Diaspora."[13]

Coleman, Roseman, and Haynes, as well as the five members of the Roots, play on one of my all-time favorite tracks, "Mellow My Man." Its addictive, head-bobbing groove has been a concert staple. Its simple hook, "It's like that for my mellow my man," with variations, is sung about 10 times in a row with Trotter and Malik B trading verses. Midway in the song, as Trotter begins his second verse, the tempo doubles, with Hubbard leading on bass, Thompson hitting a soft cymbal, and Roseman, Haynes, and Coleman swirling around each other. Trotter's rhymes are smart and funny, and, as usual, bragging. "Turn that heat down, I'm crazy cool/Deeper than the pool that Wilt the Stilt damn near drowned in," referring to 7'1" NBA star Wilt Chamberlin. Very often, when playing the song live, several of

13. https://m-base.com/what-is-m-base/.

the musicians will begin a step dance, back and forth, during the hook, their legs twisting and spinning in unison. In honor of its jazz roots, they also usually give extended instrumental improvisation space in the midst of the song.

Another beautiful tract (#29), "Swept Away," begins with a simple six-note progression on Hubbard's bass, joined after two repetitions by a descending series of notes from Coleman's sax, along with a tap-tap-tap from Thompson, playing on the side of his snare. As Trotter dives into verse one of his rhyme, jazz vocalist Casandra Wilson slides in alongside Coleman, offering a scat-like descending and rising line flowing with the rhyme, the base and drum keeping everything grooving, and the audience's head bobbing. The lyrics are, on the whole, playful bragging about what will happen to lame "MC's who slept for days," who "must be swept away." Malik B's first verse ends with this hilarious couple of braggadocios lines, "Now, you're all dessert cause I'mma serve ya like a tray/To meet your doom, Malik's the broom, so you get swept awayyyy."

The last track (33) on the album, "The Unlocking," by the Philadelphia poet and spoken word artist Ursula Rucker, turns from the playful braggadocio and head bobbing grooves to a more somber, prophetic mood. The track sets a profound political direction for the Roots, something their work to this point had only obliquely hinted at. But here, in a strikingly powerful form, is a critique of a whole genre of hip-hop just coming into being in the early 1990s represented most immediately by Andre "Dr. Dre" Young's album, *The Chronic*. *The Chronic* represents hip-hop forces emerging from the west coast in the early 1990s, so-called "gangsta rap" that among other things tended to reduce women to sexual objects. In fact, the last track on *The Chronic*, titled "Bitches Ain't Shit," has a hook, rapped by collaborator, Calvin "Snoop Dogg" Broadus Jr., that begins, "Bitches ain't shit but hoes and tricks/lick on these nuts and suck the dick." The verses, then, trade stories back and forth about various exploits with women with the explicit goal to shock. Young said in an interview at the time, "Everybody trying to do this Black power and shit, so I was like, let's give'm an alternative. Nigger nig- gerniggerniggernigger fuck this fuck that bitch bitch bitch bitch suck my dick, all this kind of shit, you know what I'm saying?"[14]

Rucker's poem is a story of a gang rape in a studio told from the perspective of the woman who, though treated as a "hoe" by the men, asserts her dignity and power over them one by one until in a surprising ending, she turns on them,

So poised, she rises

Phoenix from the flame

finally bored with their feeble fuck games

She smooth reaches behind her and takes straight aim

At eight shriveled up cocks with a fully loaded Glock

Parts lips, not expressly made for milking dicks

And then, she speaks:

Your shrieks of horror bring me bliss, I must admit

The thought that I could shred your tips with eight quick flips

Excites me, see y'all fuck with the pussy

But I fuck with your minds

Lack of soul and respect is the crime

This . . . was a set up . . . now tell me what . . . what's my name?

14. Chang, *Can't Stop, Won't Stop*, 318.

[gun cocks]

In a brilliant analysis of the track, Amherst College Associate Professor of English, Marisa Parham, makes the connection in these closing lines to Pam Grier at the end of the 1974 classic blaxploitation movie Foxy Brown. Grier poses as a prostitute to gain access to the pimp and drug lord who killed her boyfriend. Once in his presence, she reaches back into her Afro to pull out a gun, flipping the scene into her control. Further, she notes, the woman's final line, "what's my name," is "one of hip-hop's most common and well-known strategies for self-assertion," something Trotter does himself in "Essaywhuman?!!!??!" earlier on the album.[15]

Thompson says that when *The Chronic* came out, it "changed the face of hip hop." The album was a huge hit, and its production, flow, and style became a model for an emerging genre of hip-hop. It foreshadows a more direct critique of "gangsta hip hop" on their future albums, such as *Illadelph Halflife's* track "What They Do" (see chapter 3). Here, they match *The Chronic's* final track, "Bitches Ain't Shit," with "The Unlocking." Rucker offers a critique of the conspicuous consumption of some hip-hop, arguing for a division between "hip-hop" and "rap": "The major attention is given to the glamour, the rap not hip-hop. Rap music which is not hip-hop! People like The Roots and Common, Bahamadia; they all live hip-hop. They are part of the movement. They are dedicated to this way of life. Not just for the art of it but for the politics of it, for the culture of it, the changes that you can make via this movement."[16]

Historically, hip-hop is indeed not the same as rap, rap being short for rapping, MCing, the rhyming lead

15. Parham, "You Can't Flow Over This," 99.
16. Ursula Rucker, Interviewed by Stephan Oettel.

vocals so prominent for the art form, while hip-hop refers to a broader culture that includes as one of its features a kind of politically aware Afrocentric politics of the kind pioneered by Afrika Bambatta and the Native Tongues Collective. With this move, the Roots strongly place themselves in this tradition that comes to be referred to as "conscious hip hop."

These early years gave the Roots ample time to explore and play with their unfolding style. Coming out of their art school contexts, they established a trajectory of playing real instruments rather than the typical hip-hop mode of sampling from the albums of other bands. The playing, and playful engagement with their art, became a passion, something that sustained them through the hard work of making it to the point of a major label recording contract. And as they deepened this trajectory of playing together, they embrace a passion for a kind of prophetic voice, evident in various places but nowhere as clearly as "The Unlocking." Their prophetic voice emerges more clearly and strongly on their next albums, so much so that in time, as Thompson admits, "everyone just assumes that we're so serious." But, reaching back to their early and ever-present playful side, he says "I think it's possible to have a sense of humor and still be politically aware and politically and socially responsible."[17]

17. Thompson, "Roots: Getting Personal in 'How I Got Over.'"

3

"What They Do":
Passionate Commitment

After the Roots' third album *Illadelph Halflife*, Thompson bought a modest house on St. Alban Street in South Philadelphia. He and the band were beginning to imagine what was next, and he was involved in a new relationship with a neo-soul artist named Michael Archer, better known as D'Angelo. Thompson was beginning to work with him on what would become his classic album, *Voodoo*. Rich Nichols, the Roots manger, asked their new label president for some cash to put a few supportive structures in place for creative exploration—and they got it. They hired a chef, and started jam sessions at Thompson's Alban Street house, drawing on their growing network and reputation. It recalls the "The Square Roots" collective feel of their early years playing with friends on the streets and at the clubs around Philadelphia. In addition to D'Angelo, the early list of collaborators is a who's-who: Jill Scott, Bilal Sayeed Oliver, Eve Jihan Jeffers-Cooper, India Arie Simpson, James Poyser, and Lonnie Rashid Lynn

Jr., better known as Common. Lynn was starting to work on a follow-up to his 1997 *One Day It'll All Make Sense.* Thompson recalls, they "were playing loud music until all hours. But it wasn't playing loud music on boom boxes or stereos. They were actually playing it on guitars and singing with microphones . . . it was an indisputably magical time, a kind of rebirth."

Tipped off by producer Russell Elevado, D'Angelo learned that the famed Electric Lady studio in New York City built by Jimmy Hendrix was available. It had fallen into disuse and was relatively untouched since the 1970s when classic albums like Stevie Wonder's *Music of My Mind* and *Talking Book* were recorded there. Drawn to the vintage instruments and recording equipment, as well as the spiritual vibe of the studio's history, Thompson, D'Angelo, Poyser, and James Yancey, better known as J Dilla or Jay Dee, relocated their communal efforts to New York, and continued their creative passions, again drawing on a wide group of friends and collaborators. D'Angelo recalls, "We were literally blowing dust off of the Fender Rhodes that was in there," the very piano Stevie Wonder recorded on some 25 years earlier.[1]

Soon, Thompson also convinced Common to join them to record what became *Like Water for Chocolate*, and the Roots began recording their own next album, *Things Fall Apart*. Sometimes, they were recording simultaneously in three different rooms at Electric Lady. All of them were inspired by J Dilla's particular style of beats, "like someone drunk was playing drums," or, as Thompson reaches for an adequate description, "a drunk, brilliant four-year-old

1. Chinen, "How The Soulquarians Birthed D'Angelo's 'Voodoo' and Transformed Jazz."

43

has been allowed to program the kick drum pattern."[2] In addition, desiring to draw lessons from the greats, they analyzed albums and live concert videos from Prince, Stevie Wonder, and older jazz, funk, and soul artists. Calling these their "Yoda" figures, they often took an oblique feel from an artist or album into recording, rather than a more direct use of a sample, or doing a straightforward remake of a classic song. The producer, Elevado, described what brought them all together: "All these people had a vision [that] stems from these hip-hop grooves—and it's coming out of the old '70s funk records, and R&B."[3]

One day, Thompson discovered that four members of the group that had gathered around Electric Lady had birthdays in late January and February, putting them under the sign of Aquarius, and, he recalls, "in the course of joking around someone invented the idea of the Soulquarians." Other friends joined in on each other's sessions—and soon they'd drawn in Erykah Badu, who came to record her album *Mama's Gun*, along with other friends: Dante Terrell Smith, known at the time as Mos Def (and now as Yaslin Bey); his musical partner, Talib Kweli, as well as Jonathan William Davids, known as Q-Tip (who has also changed his name, to Kamaal Ibn John Fareed), Raphael Saadiq, the trumpter Roy Hargrove, and many others. Unfortunately, the collective unraveled prematurely after a feature article ran in *Vibe* magazine attributing the collective solely to Thompson, as if the other artists worked for him. It was the opposite of his intention, as Vibe initially proposed an article just on him, and he convinced them to focus on the collective. Despite its short life, the collective had a huge influence, with its members scoring multiple

2. Thompson, *Mo' Meta Blues*, 159.
3. Chinen, "How The Soulquarians Birthed D'Angelo's 'Voodoo.'"

gold and platinum albums, Grammy awards, and more. They are still influential, as jazz critic Nate Chinen argues in his recent book *Playing Changes: Jazz for the New Century*. He points out that in part due to the dynamic interplay of the Soulquarians, single categories like jazz or soul or hip-hop don't work adequately for new artists such as Kamazi Washington, Esperanza Spalding, Robert Glasper, or Vijay Iyer.[4]

Kneeling, front left: Common, front right: J Dilla. Standing, left to right: Talib Kweli, Mos Def, James Poyser, Erykah Badu, Amhir "Questlove" Thompson, D'Angelo, Q-Tip, and Bilal

God and Passion

Unfolding this opening vignette about the development of the Soulquarians shows an example of how the "play" of the Roots early years turned into a "passion"—and perhaps for Thompson—an obsessive one! Tony Wagner, as I described earlier, argues for the central importance of an extended period of play in which a context is set for exploring—and finding—one's gifts. The first period of

4. Chinen, *Playing Changes*.

play opens into a second period marked by passion, digging into those areas that, in the midst of play, children discover themselves to be both very good at something, and often for that very reason, also to find it deeply joyful. The point is certainly not to say, play begins here, and passion follows. In fact, the reality is that play continues to be a crucial component all along, and passion is a result of self-knowledge about one's gifts, and thereby focusing in on specific modes of play that bring joy and satisfaction.

As I turn to think briefly about God and passion, I want to lean more in the direction of that kind of embodied joy and satisfaction of finding one's place, one's people, rather than the typical theological exploration of passion that looks to the so-called "passion" of Jesus. I do not discount the importance of the suffering, trial, and crucifixion of Jesus by the rulers of his age—what is usually meant by Jesus' passion. In fact, it can play a crucial role in thinking about, as James Cone has show us, contemporary issues of racial justice, insofar as the cross and the lynching tree are but two modes of the same repressive, state-sanctioned mob violence.[5] But here, I'm more interested in passion on an everyday human level, and of the kind that draws us into community, in the process transforming ourselves through passionate engagement with others.

Charles Taylor has shown how a certain Western philosophical tradition privileged Greek notions of moderation and dispassionate reason over against embodiment and emotional engagement.[6] Key to his argument is the biblical witness to Jesus' compassion that drew him not only to know more deeply his own calling but into relationship with those who were suffering, those he most felt

5. Cone, *Cross and the Lynching Tree*.
6. Taylor, *Secular Age*, 278; Scharen, "Eclipsing."

called to serve. As Willie James Jennings shows, it was just this philosophical tradition that also developed a series of structures of racial, class, and gender distinction showing reasonable white men to be superior to all others who are too driven by their passions, their emotions, and thereby are more like children or even animals, in need of direction, leadership, and discipline. At its worst this twisted system led to declaring whole groups of people (Native peoples, Africans) as savage, not fully human.[7] Jesus, however, is shown over and over again doing the opposite: claiming those despised and disregarded by the rich and powerful as valued and as fully human, as children of God.

In Mark's Gospel, the earliest of the Gospels, Jesus goes to a secluded place to rest and eat with his disciples. A crowd sees him go, and runs to the place, arriving before him. Mark 6:34 (NRSV) reads, "As he went ashore, he saw a great crowd; and he had compassion for them, because they were like sheep without a shepherd." The Greek word here for compassion, as Charles Taylor points out in his critique of the philosophical traditions of *apatheia* or the absence of passion, is *splagchnizomai*. This is an embodied term meaning "to be moved in one's guts," which were thought to be the source of love and compassion in the body.[8] And again and again, Jesus is drawn to those "without a shepherd," those, that is, who were in need.

But that is not the only way Jesus' passion works itself out in relationship to those in need. His meal practices bring passion and joy, especially for those who were considered the outcasts of his day. In fact, he was so well-known for this practice that he became famous for it. The rulers of the day asked his followers, "Why does your teacher eat with

---

7. Taylor, *Secular Age*, 115; Jennings, *Christian Imagination.*
8. Taylor, *Secular Age*, 115.

tax collectors and sinners?" (Mark 2:16). In John's Gospel, at the wedding at Cana, Jesus' first miracle is to turn water into wine after the wine runs out. And it is the best wine! (John 2). In fact, it might be possible to argue Jesus really finds the fullness of his mission through meals with those he is not supposed to be eating with. Those meals vary—some one-on-one, some with a small group, and at times with large gatherings of thousands. Of course, some of Jesus' most deeply important meals are with his closest disciples.

In her fantastic book *Divine Enjoyment: A Theology of Passion and Exuberance*, Latinx theologian Elaine Padilla offers a much-needed intervention in the Christian tradition too long weighted down by a heresy parading as orthodoxy—that passion, pleasure, or unfettered joy are bad and sinful. Yet, she argues, following the writings of sociologist Otto Maduro on "la buena vida" and "las fiestas," that a passion for others, and meals enjoyed in their presence, is core to the "life abundant" to which God invites us in Christ. "The thief comes only to steal and kill and destroy," Jesus says in John 10:10. "I came that you might have life, and have it abundantly." Padilla quotes Maduro:

> But the life that we long for and treasure is one to be lived abundantly: life that is possible to enjoy together with others without putting in peril that others might also enjoy it . . . the good life— the life that deserves to be preserved, nourished, communicated, reproduced and celebrated—is the shared enjoyment of affect, the company, the labor, the food, the art, the game, the prayer, the dance . . . the celebration.[9]

9. Padilla, *Divine Enjoyment*, 1.

In the original Spanish, Maduro ends this beautiful sentiment: "¡y la fiesta!" Life, Padilla suggests, is in the Christian
view more than merely survival, and certainly more than
suffering. A key vision of eternal life is, in fact, a banquet,
a heavenly fiesta (cf. Luke 22:16; Matt 26:29).

Padilla not only challenges the cultural ideal of in-
dividualism and self-sufficiency so often held up as the
model of what it means to be happy—to depend on none
but oneself. She also challenges the historical Christian
theological notion called "divine impassibility—or *apatheia*"—the notion that God is not moved, and can't in
fact be moved, by the passions of the world God has made.
This notion was developed, as I mention above, out of the
merger of Western theology and Greek philosophy, and it
is a wholly unbiblical argument. Major twentieth-century
theologians, and especially of the liberationist school, like
Jon Sobrino and Jurgen Moltmann, have challenged this
notion. They argue compellingly that God feels and responds to the suffering of the world. In fact, if Jesus is God,
the second person of the Trinity, then his own suffering
and death happens as an event internal to the life of God. It
is also possible, then, Padilla argues, to understand God as
experiencing delight, passion, desire for the creation and
creatures with whom God is in an unfolding relationship.
As a feminist, she turns to the example of birth, of creating
new life, most certainly a key feature of God's work and
the work of women in the world. There is suffering, pain,
yes, and yet life is also both joyful and hopeful, entailing a
vision of a good future yet to come, as yet unknown, but
glimpsed even now.[10]

In Padilla's work, a generative vision of God and
passion emerges, with a biblical and theological claim

10. Padilla, *Divine Enjoyment,* 12–13.

about the role of passionate engagement with others, and of finding one's own generative role in being with others in life-giving ways. From this, a powerful communal image emerges: of a celebration, a meal, of a "fiesta," and of creation, of new birth, within a larger frame of accountability to those who are suffering, those on the bottom of the social order. The spirit of these theological modes fit with the increasingly communal and socially conscious work of the Roots in this next phase of their development. They develop a more explicitly prophetic voice, in part as I hinted at in the previous chapter, by way of contrast to the emerging commercialization of another kind of hip hop—the kind represented by *The Chronic*, and what followed from it. More on that in the pages to follow.

The Passion of the Roots

The Roots' third album emerged from the disappointment with their major label debut, an effort that received some critical praise but wasn't commercially successful. Both of their albums to date followed the pattern of their emergence as a jazz-oriented hip-hop collective that frankly was better live than recorded. They admitted they didn't know how to write pop songs, and hadn't really worried about it because they naively thought their artistry would win the day, not only with their hardcore fans, but with a wider audience. When this proved not to be the case, and with full consideration of the wider and changing hip-hop scene, they now knew much more intimately. They knew they needed a different sort of album. Thompson reflects, "We didn't want to be as soft as we were on the earlier record, but we didn't want to surrender our thinking man's perch, either." It was, in music, lyrics, the album cover, the first single and its video, "Clones," shot entirely on urban streets, a look and feel intended to shore up their cred as hip-hop artists in a changing climate.

Illadelph Halflife was released in September 1996, just two weeks after the shooting death of Tupac Shakur in Las Vegas. Shakur was one of the leading west-coast rappers associated with gangsta rap although his diverse and powerful body of work can't simply be reduced to a stereotype.[11] The rise of this form of hip-hop, emerging from neighborhoods in Los Angeles like Compton, Watts, and South Central, goes hand-in-hand with a west-coast mirror of the social abandonment experienced in the Bronx a decade earlier, and the alternative economy of drugs and crime fueled by the introduction of crack cocaine. In the late 1970s and 1980s, major manufacturing plants closed (more that 100 shuttered during the decade in Los Angeles alone) leaving high unemployment and poverty rates.[12] At the same time, "Freeway" Ricky Ross's 1980s cocaine empire turned from expensive powder form to cheap "freebase" or "crack" cocaine, devastating poor neighborhoods, and spreading like wildfire spread from Los Angeles to every major city in the US. Ross's Nicaraguan supplier was involved in the CIA's anti-communist efforts in Central America, using cocaine sales to fund Contra rebels fighting there. Policing, especially targeting gangs as code for youth of color, spread among law enforcement. L.A.'s Operation Hammer, the development of "three strikes" laws, and many similar efforts were part of a larger "politics of containment" as in most 1980s cities, white elders tried to govern majority populations of

---

11. On Tupac, see Hodge, *Heaven has a Ghetto* and *Baptized in Dirty Water,* among many others.

12. Chang, *Can't Stop, Won't Stop*, 314.

black and brown youth.[13] In a real sense, these moves were the beginnings of what Michelle Alexander, decades later, called "the new Jim Crow" as a description of the system of mass incarceration.[14]

Unfortunately, the social protest of gangsta rap, aimed at police and the broader dominant white culture, is too often overlooked. Shakur's death represents another side of the culture of that moment—caught in the devolution of hip-hop into its own violence, fueled by money, competition, and rivalry. Thompson describes this spiral of violence as the death of hip-hop as he understood it. The primary lines of rivalry were between the so-called west-coast hip-hop of Death Row records led by Marion Hugh "Suge" Knight, with Andre "Dr. Dre" Young as his most famous recording artist, and east coast hip-hop of Bad Boy records led by Sean "Puffy" Combs whose big artist at the time, Christopher Wallace, was known as The Notorious B.I.G., Biggie Smalls, or just Biggie. Recalling the infamous *Source* Magazine Hip-Hop Awards ceremony earlier that year in New York, Thompson narrates the competition for awards between the two biggest albums that year, a more old-school inner-city coming of age album by Nasir "Nas" bin Olu Dara Jones, *Illmatic*, and a new gangsta rap album by Biggie called *Born to Die*. As the night wore on, Thompson recalls, Biggie won all the awards, and the atmosphere was like a powder-keg, menacing enough that he ran for the exit fearing shooting would break out.

The Philadelphia Inquirer's review of *Illadelph Half-life* called it the "first release in the post-Tupac Shakur era in rap," and noted that the album shows "how far-reaching and how far removed from the gangsta stereotype hip-hop

13. Chang, *Can't Stop, Won't Stop*, 387.

14. Alexander, *New Jim Crow*.

can be."[15] In fact, some of the early songs on the album both decry and lament such violence on the streets. Track 37, "Panic!!!" starts softly with tambourine shaking and a slight wavering keyboard, but at the twenty second mark, the full band comes in forcefully as Trotter raps, "I woke up in the darkness at 12:17 . . . to shots and sirens" and unfolds in detail the shooting of a young man on his street who was into selling crack. Trotter recalls, "I tried to tell to stop cuz yo, its ghetto red hot/similar to the blood now floodin his top." His rhymes twist between lament and anger and protest: "Damn, I'm thinkin it don't cease, it's no more peace/Police level increase, but what the fuck/Its still crime on the streets/I can't breathe, now what's goin on?/One minute you alive, the next, you're gone/Illadel-P-H-I-A Hell." It is not just every genre of hip-hop, but for that matter most genres of black music, that critique the omnipresent reality of racist policing, from Grandmaster Flash and the Furious Five's "The Message" all the way up to Kendrick Lamar's Pulitzer-Prize-winning 2017 album *DAMN.* or Childish Gambino's viral 2018 hit song and video, "This is America."

The very next track, "It Just Don't Stop" picks up the theme with a despairing hook: "Dig it, this world is filled with homicides and rape / All the crimes of hate just ain't the size and shape / You can walk down the block and get slumped or knocked / It don't stop y'all, and it just don't stop (dig it) (come with it)." Malik B and Trotter trade verses, telling the truth as they see it, each verse ending with a call to another approach to survival than that of guns, "That's why I walk around with my brain on cock." The album includes a new keyboardist, James "Kamal" Gray, at the time still in high school, and who has remained a

15. Thompson, *Mo' Meta Blues*, 144.

steady member ever since. The album also includes some guests from their previous album including jazz musicians Joshua Redman, Steve Coleman, Cassandra Wilson, and Graham Haynes. A proto-Soulquarians group of musical influences also show up, with tracks featuring Philadelphia rappers Dice Raw, Bahamadia, Q-Tip, and Ursula Rucker, but also new friends like D'Angelo, Common, and Raphael Saadiq.

Perhaps the most infamous song (and video) from the album, track 41 "What They Do," features Raphael Saadiq, a smooth R&B artist whose groove singing the hook adds to the overall easy feel of the song. But the easy groove masks the way the song represents a direct challenge to the likes of Dr. Dre, Biggie, and other artists who embrace the gangsta style and cashed in as a result (ironically, as I note above, from a largely white fan base). One of Biggie's singles from *Born to Die*, titled "One More Chance," sold more than a million copies that year alone. The song, about his sexual prowess, was matched with a video of a fancy party at his home with lots of champagne and scantily-clad women dancing, and Biggie rapping on the side of a bed with another woman, also wearing very little, obviously meant to be waiting for him. The Roots song, "What They Do," doesn't directly reference Biggie, or any hip-hop artists, but does take on the shifting culture of hip-hop. "The principles of true hip-hop have been forsaken/It's all contractual and about money makin." "Yo, I dedicate this to the one-dimensional/No imagination, excuse for perpetration." It is a bold throw-down, delivered in their classic style, with their band in full swing, adding excellent jazz guitar from Spanky Alford, and Angela Slates joining Saadiq on the simple, devastating hook. "Never do . . . what they do, what they do, what they do."

While the song was already a bold intervention in the internal debates over the future of hip hop, it was the video that really pushed the envelope and created serious bad blood. Their director had just done a video for their label-mates, Tesla, whose video had subtitles explaining each part of the video in the context of the whole, and by doing so, satirically deconstructing the idea of the music video itself. The Roots took this to another level, using this convention to make fun of "all those rap-video clichés that were prevalent at the time." The video opens showing the band driving up to a mansion (subtitle: rented for the day) in a black BMW sedan (subtitle: first 100 miles free) and inside, they host a party including women dancing in bikinis (subtitle: the money shot, automatic record sales), and of course, lots of champagne (subtitle: its really ginger ale). It turns out, the video included many scenes that were very similar to Biggie's "One More Chance" video, including the shot with Trotter sitting on the side of a bed with a woman in bed, and then two women, and in the next shot, three women, all with champagne glasses, wearing bikinis (subtitle: yeah, right). It was, in retrospect, no surprise that Biggie was mad, and said so publicly. As soon as they heard, Thompson penned a long op-ed piece defending their critique of the way hip-hop had become over-commercialized and distant from its own community. However, before they could respond, tragically, Biggie was shot, thought by many as payback for Tupac's shooting earlier that year, in which Wallace was rumored to have been involved. (While never published due to Biggie's death, very similar themes show up in the series Thompson published in 2014 on vulture.com, an online magazine, titled, "How Hip Hop Failed Black America.") What felt like satire now felt like tragedy. It must have been little consolation, but when Thompson later was first introduced to Prince, he said, "I know who he is, I love that ["What They Do"] video!"[16]

The passion for their art, for hip-hop as they believed in it, you might say, drew them to satirize a movement within hip-hop they felt was literally going to kill off hip-hop. Thompson said as much, calling the second *Source* awards when Biggie won all the awards and so much bad blood was in the room, a literal funeral for hip-hop. To be sure, commercial rap would go on, but it wouldn't be the same as what had inspired their passion in the first place. However, already with *Illadelph Halflife*, the group that would become the Soulquarians was coalescing and, as the opening of the chapter describes, this collective of like-minded musicians felt like a new birth for the Roots, if not for hip-hop as a whole. The creative energy of this group of musicians, all working on their own albums and, in a kind of studio-level improvisation, all working on each other's albums as well, was catalyzing. All this passion for their art, and the relationships, the community, they were forming, deeply impacted the leap they made as a band on their next album.

In picking album titles, the Roots developed the idea of an album title being a threefold commentary: on what was happening for the band, for hip-hop, and society more generally.[17] *Things Fall Apart*, the title of their next, and to date most successful studio album, is an obvious play on the Chinua Achebe novel. The novel is a story about Nigeria and the constant change as old traditions are washed away by the new Western colonial ways. It resonated with the band members as an analogy for the Roots, and for hip-hop in general. Thompson: "We were part of a music

16. Thompson, *Mo' Meta Blues*, 142.
17. Thompson, *Mo' Meta Blues*, 202.

that had, at least early on, been so new, so true to itself, but there had been a corruption from the outside and what was once there was gone." Without overstating the case, they felt it was a blues album, drawing on Ralph Ellison's definition of the blues as an "autobiographical chronicle of a personal catastrophe expressed lyrically."[18] They felt the same about society, so the album was released originally with five variant covers each with a historical photo representing different social ills: famine, violence, discrimination, and fear. Art Director Kenny Gravillis, who has designed numerous Roots album covers, worked with the band to find the right photos—all that visually represent a "failure in society—humanity in its darkest hour." The most affecting, they felt, and resonant for the album became the main cover. The photographer and people in the photograph remain unknown, but the photo depicts white police in the late 1960s chasing two black teenagers in the Bedford-Stuyvesant section of Brooklyn, New York. The look of real terror on the girls' face is powerful, and surely, for an urban Black audience then and now, all too imaginable.[19]

18. Thompson, *Mo' Meta Blues*, 165.
19. Dryden, "Art Director Kenny Gravillis."

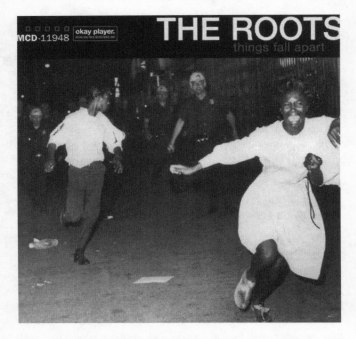

The opening of the album is telling on a number of levels. It is track 54 in their body of work now stretching back over four albums, and is called "Act Won (Things Fall Apart)." As a sideways way of reflecting on the tensions in hip-hop, they include a snippet of dialog from Spike Lee's 1990 film, *Mo' Better Blues*. Bleek Gilliam, played by Denzel Washington, is a frustrated jazz purist who doesn't understand the lack of support from his own black community. He reflects, "If we had to depend upon black people to eat, we would starve to death. I mean, you've been out there, you're on the bandstand, you look out into the audience, what do you see? You see Japanese, you see West Germans . . . anything except our own people. It makes no sense. It incenses me that our own people don't realize our own heritage, our own culture. This is our music, man!" He is

talking to Shadow Henderson, played by Wesley Snipes, a
hotheaded young sax player in the band who has his own
ideas. His quickly offered retort is, "That's bullshit. Everything you just said is bullshit . . . That's right, the people
don't come because you grandiose motherfuckers don't
play shit that they like. If you played the shit that they like,
then the people would come, simple as that."[20]

A few tracks early on seem to follow this logic, with
track 56, "The Next Movement," written by new keys player
Kamal Gray, and featuring a solid line by Gray and Hubbard holding the song in motion, and Philly hometown
hero Jeffery Allen Townes, known as DJ Jazzy Jeff, one half
of the successful collaboration with musician and actor
Will Smith, The Fresh Prince. With Townes doing scratch,
and another Philly group, Tracey Moore and Mercedes
Martinez, known as the Jazzyfatnastees singing backup
vocals, Trotter's strong rhymes have their match. Claiming
their mantle as artists for social change, Trotter announces
"That's how we usually start/Once again it's the Thought/
The Dalai Lama of the mic/The prime minister Thought."
He continues: "This directed to whoever in listening range
/ Yo the whole state of things in the world bout to change
/ Black rain fallin from the sky look strange / The ghetto
is red hot, we steppin on flames." The bridge seeks to en-
list the listener to make a change: "Hey you listeners, stop
what you're doin and / Set it in motion, it's the next movement." The song was the fourth single off the album, and is
a standout track

As I noted above, J Dilla had a deep influence on
the album—and the whole atmosphere at the Electric
Lady studios shaping a series of ground-breaking albums.
Dilla produced what to this day is my favorite track on

20. Lee, *Mo' Better Blues.*

this album, track 59, "Dynamite!" Its infectious guitar, bass, and drum groove literally makes the body move. The fantastic guitarist on the track, Anthony Tidd, is an interesting story of the fruit of the Roots' passion for the collective, and not the the individual, mode for making music. Through musical innovator and saxophonist Steve Coleman, who played on the Roots' early albums, the group met Tidd, a bass and guitar player as well as composer and producer. Of Trinidadian background, Tidd grew up in London, getting formal training in music and joining a number of experimental groups there. The story is, when Coleman first met Tidd, recruiting him for a project, he popped in a tape with drums, and Tidd, blown away, said, "Who is that!" Coleman said, "A guy in Philly named Amir Thompson." The Roots lived with Tidd during a stint in London, and then helped him transition to the US, where he's developed an amazing footprint playing with Coleman and on many other projects. No doubt, these same circles led, just a few years later, to another fantastic guitarist via a Coleman connection, "Captain" Kirk Douglas, who has remained a core member from 2002 on. More on Douglas later.

Two tracks in the middle of the album are each, in their own ways, paying homage to hip-hop. The track Thompson calls the centerpiece of the album, track 62, "Double Trouble" feat. Mos Def, didn't start out well. Thompson recalls being out with friends each producing new material, and they shared clips with each other. The first two were enthusiastically praised, but when Thompson played the demo of "Double Trouble," their perfunctory head-bobbing devastated him. He remembers going straight back to the studio, and working until he had redone the song top to bottom, significantly upping his game. In the end, he took it as a gift, albeit a hard one to swallow. Yet the lesson stuck, and thereafter, he had more clearly in mind not just the critics, but his producer peers, and more generally, the listening audience.

The track draws on old-school hip-hop: "Stoop Rap/ Double Trouble," from a scene in Wild Style, a famous old-school hip hop film from 1983. Trouble KK RockWell and LiL Rodney C, from the group Funky 4+1, are seen in the movie sitting on a stoop of a brownstone in the South Bronx, trading verses back and forth. Trotter and Mos Def do the same thing, clearly having fun with the playfulness of the rhythms. In Mos Def's last verse, he says: "It's just me and Tariq, with Ahmir on the beat / The Roots crew baby yo we got to make it unique / We got the soul-shockinest, body-rockinest / Non-stoppinest, Fortified Live survive the apocalypse / Rhymes we say, the perfect blend / Because we know how to rock when the beat come in."

While "Double Trouble" shows their love for hip-hop and its history, the next track (63) makes it explicit. With the help of Common, "Act Too (The Love of my Life)", feat. Common on a verse, the song just puts it out there: "Hip hop, you the love of my life/I'm bout to take you to the top." Yet in a love song to the hip-hop they love, they couldn't resist throwing a jab at the hip-hop they don't: "Her Daddy'll beat H.E.R., eyes all Puff-ed/In the mix on tape, niggas had her in the buff/When we touch, it was more that just a fuck/The Police." The references to Sean "Puff Daddy" Combs, the producer behind Biggie, and NWA, Dr. Dre's original group, are unmistakable.

But if Things Fall Apart is known for a song, it is "You Got Me" feat. Erykah Badu and Eve (track 68). It won the Root's first Grammy award, and was a significant reason the album is considered as the Root's "breakthrough album." Originally written with the Roots' Philly friend and fellow artist, Jill Scott, they shifted from Scott when their label wanted a higher-profile singer for the hook, and with Badu already at Electric Lady working on her own album, *Mama's Gun*, she was a natural. The track features beautiful guitar work from Tidd and what Thompson calls a "dirty" drum beat, off-kilter and drunk-sounding (learned from J. Dilla). Hubbard and Gray, along with guest string players, join in laying down a slow-burning tune, helping define the emerging "neo-soul" movement. The song, a back and forth between a hip hop boyfriend (Trotter) and photographer girlfriend (Eve), deals with the tensions of being apart, on the road, and the strains on the relationship. With Badu singing the hook, she assures her "boo" that "Baby, don't worry, You know that you got me." While Scott's version of the hook didn't make the record, she toured with the Roots, taking that chance, night by night, to reclaim the song she helped to develop in the beginning.

As with the last two albums, *Things Fall Apart* ends with a powerful spoken word poem by Ursula Rucker, "The Return to Innocence Lost." The track starts with the innocence sound of what seems like a child's wind-up toy, its little bell tune slowly playing as the toy turns. This innocence is lost with Rucker's first words, "Muffled sound of fist on flesh/Blows to chest/No breath/Air gasps." Thompson describes the poem: "It's about violence in an interracial marriage, the tragedy of asking children to look up to a man who isn't prepared to be a father. It's about choices made in life, as wrong as often as they're right . . . " The woman, in whose voice the poem unfolds, has children in the midst of her abusive, troubled relationship, and as her first-born son grows, unable to "protect

Mommy's neck from Daddy's grasp," or "shield her ears from/Daddy's foul-mouthed, liquor-breath jeers," he connects with street life, getting in all sorts of trouble till December 24 when he is shot and killed while picking up drugs with a "False Friend" from a "suburban supplier": "Hit . . . Lost Boy in back/So-called Friend runs for door/ Leaves First Son blood-born/Lying alone in blood on cold floor/Death was the cost of . . . /Returning to Innocence Lost . . . "

4

"How I Got Over":
Purpose in Prime Time

I f the Soulquarians were a rebirth for the Roots in the late
1990s, then meeting Jimmy Fallon was another sort of
rebirth in the late 2000s. The basic story has been told so
many times, it has become mythic. Fallon had gotten the
nod to take Conan O'Brien's chair as host of *Late Night*,
and was trying to figure out what to do for a band on the
show. He ran into Neal Brennan, co-creator of the Dave
Chappelle show. Fallon: "I said to him, who could be the
band, the band is going to be very important on the show,
and he said, you should ask the Roots, and I was like, you
think the Roots would do it?!, and he was like, (crinkle
face), No! but they might know someone who would do it,
they're very nice people." A few weeks later, in Los Angeles
for a Roots show at UCLA, Thompson ran into Fallon, and
the conversation quickly turned to the request. Thompson
said, "Maybe," and invited him to the show. After the show,
Thompson says, recalling the incident in conversation with
Fallon live on *The Tonight Show*: "I was backstage doing an

interview, and when I walked out of my dressing room, you (Fallon) had managed to get those guys (points across the studio to the Roots) to get in that 'Eight Is Enough' human pyramid, even Tariq, everything that Tariq wears is like 9 thousand dollars (Fallon, Trotter and the Roots crew all laughing), I'm just saying that for the fact that Tariq was on the bottom row, on UCLA grass, and I said to my manager, we're not getting rid of this guy."[1]

A *Tonight Show* bit with Jimmy Fallon and the Roots playing Carly Rae Jepson's song "Call Me Maybe" with only elementary school classroom instruments.

But there is a back story on this moment and the stakes, both for Jimmy Fallon and for the Roots, too. Fallon had grown up in New York completely fixated on *Saturday Night Live*. Skilled as a musician and a comic, he began recording and recreating sketches from the show in high school, and eventually dropped out of college to move to Los Angeles to do stand up. After one failed audition attempt for SNL, he redoubled his efforts, saying, "It's crazy,

---

1. Fallon, "Questlove Remembers When Jimmy Won The Roots Over."

I had no other plan!" When he finally got a chance to audition again, he did so well that head writer Tina Fey said he was "one of two people I've ever seen who was completely ready to be on the show . . . like if there had been a show to do that night." Crucially, his imitations—especially of Adam Sandler, who had just left the show—made show creator Lorne Michaels laugh, a rarity. Fallon became a star on SNL, becoming close to Michaels in the process. But Fallon left SNL for a film career that didn't go well at all (his first film, *Taxi,* was a critical and popular flop). Michaels, however, had his eye on Fallon for the *Late Night* host role once Conan O'Brien stepped down, and he persisted in this vision despite NBC executives who were unconvinced. Given that it had been four years since Fallon left SNL, Michaels sent him on an eight-month comedy tour of college campuses to recapture his comic mojo. It was in this fraught career moment that Fallon reached out to the Roots.

For the Roots' part, starting with *Phrenology,* the 2002 follow-up to *Things Fall Apart,* the band released albums like clockwork every two years: *The Tipping Point* (2004), *Game Theory* (2006), and *Rising Down* (2008). *Rising Down* was hailed as their best album since *Things Fall Apart,* and Thompson recalls that, "even though Robert Christgau [reviewer for the New York Times] gave the record an A, for the first time I didn't feel like we were earning good grades. I felt like we were teaching the class."[2] Besides, Thompson continues, "After swimming in purgatory for fifteen years, we were making a steady living, and I didn't think I could turn my back on that."[3] If that were the only story, however, I'm not sure how to explain the Roots'

2. Thompson, *Mo' Meta Blues,* 243–44.

3. Thompson, *Mo' Meta Blues,* 243–44.

saying "yes" to Fallon's invitation. In another interview, Thompson gives more texture that helps make sense of the shift. The band were in the twentieth year, not teens any longer hanging out at each other's houses until all hours of the night. They were getting married, having kids, and the fact that they were still dependent on touring as their job created tensions for the members.

Thompson says they found themselves looking for "a Celine Dion situation" (who negotiated a standing concert series at The Colosseum hotel in Las Vegas). In 2006, the Roots seriously considered an ongoing gig at The Borgata in Atlantic City. However, Thompson quips, "I personally just felt like the Wikipedia page in my mind didn't want to end there."[4] Fallon came to the party with the band after the ULCA concert, and at a certain point, as he was joking with some of the band, Trotter pulled Thompson aside, and said, "I think I can see this happening," and Thompson replied that he could, too.[5]

God and Purpose

From the perspective of the current moment, late night television was a dynamic move for both Fallon and the Roots. However, there is a larger social purpose to be discerned in the Roots' move to late night as well. As you'll remember, the Roots choose album titles that reflect their own circumstances, those of hip-hop, and of the wider world, too. This choice to join forces with Jimmy Fallon and *Late Night*, and then *The Tonight Show*, fits that pattern. It felt like a chance to exhale for the band, to have a steady "9–5" so to speak rather than depending on touring

4. Chafin, "Man of Many Names."
5. Thompson, *Mo' Meta Blues*, 246.

for months on end to make their living: "The Fallon show is a day job in the best sense. We're in by noon and gone by seven, and in between we make a show." It also was a response to a certain kind of stagnation in hip-hop generally, and their own desire for a creative left turn. Richard Nichols, the Roots' long-time manager (who tragically died of leukemia in 2014 at the young age of 55), commenting on the creative death of hip-hop, says this: "Listen, man. The other day I heard that new 2 Chainz record, and it's a fucking object lesson in thematic narrowness, one dumbass idea repeated over and over again. There's a song called, 'Crack,' and then a song called, 'Dope Peddler,' right next to each other. Then a little later there's a song called 'I Lov Dem Strippers.'"[6] Like so much gangsta rap, such albums are almost cardboard figures, as Jeff Chang puts it, "inflated stereotypes to their breaking point—equal parts urban threat, hypersexualized Black males, and class clown."[7]

Given where the Roots felt they were at this stage in their careers, the transition to work with Fallon made sense. As they noted after their last album, *Rising Down*, they were not just trying to get good grades from the critics, but instead were teaching the class, showing how it's done.[8] And the Fallon gig gave the Roots an influential classroom, not only for hip-hop, but for American culture and the wider world. And that's the third way joining late night made sense: it worked for them personally, and in terms of hip-hop culture, as a kind of exhale and rebirth. For the broader society, though, it represented a watershed, and even more so as Fallon and the Roots moved

6. Thompson, *Mo' Meta Blues*, 152. Nichols is referring to Tauheed "2 Chainz" Epps 2012 album, *Based on a T.R.U.E. Story* (Def Jam Records).

7. Chang, *Can't Stop, Won't Stop*, 318.

8. Chang, *Can't Stop, Won't Stop*, 244.

to *The Tonight Show*, arguably the biggest platform for a musical group in television. As Trotter rhymes in "Doing It Again" from 2010's *How I Got Over*: "Dear diary, the fans still swear by me/ Even though I'm Late Night now like 'Here's Johnny'/Swimming with them Great Whites now, that's where to find me." Despite saying "yes" to the opportunity, that lyric is ambivalent, at best. The "even though" acknowledges that taking the *Late Night* gig damages their street cred from the hip-hop side, "selling out" as it were. And the swimming with "them Great Whites" suggests worries about the other side, pointing both to the cutthroat world of television, and to the fact that it is literally populated with a lot of powerful white people, including Fallon himself!

Through the 2000s, the band gradually gained a broader platform, significantly aided by their breakthrough with *Things Fall Apart*, and then their leap into late-night television. I see this gaining of a broad public platform as integral for their purpose as a band. In the framing I'm drawing on from Harvard education professor Tony Wagner, play leads to finding passion, a focusing of play around one's gifts and joy. Yet that in itself is not the full maturity of the journey, a journey that only matures in finding one's purpose, one's calling. That next step, Wagner argues, often comes while exploring a passion, as people begin to see how the world might need their gifts, and how it might matter to the world to use them. This third stage unfolds as an intentional paring of one's gifts and the world's deep need, offering a sense of purpose in the world. It leads to an existential center, a kind of grounding self-knowledge about what one is good at, and a kind of satisfaction that that thing is needed, that one can make a difference for good. This is just what the Roots came to grasp in this period, claiming their role not only as passionate strivers, as Thompson put it, but as the teachers, letting loose with their particular mode of playful, prophetic hip-hop and enjoying the highest levels of critical regard and success. It is about, as the theological reflection to follow points out, reading the signs of the times, and seeing that you've been prepared for a particular purpose, or, as the biblical story of Esther puts it, "for such a time as this."

The story of Esther might be one place to go in Scripture for thinking about prophets and purpose. It is a remarkable story in which Esther, a Jew, is chosen to be wife of the Persian king Ahasuerus. With the help of her cousin, Mordecai, she uses her position to foil the plans of the king's chief advisor, Haman, to have all the Jews in the kingdom killed. Her bravery, and savvy, to risk speaking the truth in the face of her own—and her people's—peril showed the hand of God in her place and role as wife of the king at a time of grave threats for her people. Womanist biblical scholar Wil Gafney, in her book *Daughters of Miriam: Women Prophets in Ancient Israel,* follows the rabbinic tradition in Judaism by including Esther in the group of women prophets whose stories need to be recovered as the true prophets and friends of God they were.[9] I am aware of debates about who counts as a "womanist" scholar and what distinguishes "womanist" scholarship. Nyasha Junior notes that while Gafney draws on womanist frameworks for her work, *Daughter of Miriam* "does not use a woman's approach."[10]

Gafney also lifts up Deborah, whose story is detailed in the book of Judges, chapter 4, in the Hebrew Bible. King Jabin of Canaan reigns over the Israelites, and, the story

9. Gafney, *Daughters of Miriam.*

10. Junior, *Introduction to Womanist Biblical Interpretation,* 115.

says, Sisera, the commander of King Jabin's army, had nine hundred chariots and because he had "cruelly oppressed the Israelites for twenty years, they cried to God for help." Deborah, unique in Scripture in this respect, is introduced as both a prophet and a judge, a local governor of a sort. She calls for her military leader, Barak, to lead their army against Sisera and King Jabin's army, pledging to go with him, each leading a flank of the attack, but assuring him the final glory of victory would not be his, but that of a woman. Not long after the battle begins, Sisera saw the tide turn badly against him, and he flees on foot and, finding the camp of Heber, the Kenite, hides in the tent with Heber's wife, Jael. After offering him milk and a blanket, he bides her stand in the doorway and tell anyone who comes that no one is inside. As he sleeps, Jael takes a hammer and tent peg, and quietly drives the peg through his temple into the ground, killing him, the final nail, so to speak, in their victory that day. Judges chapter 5 is a hymn of victory sung by Deborah and Barak, thought to be perhaps the oldest such poem or hymn in Scripture. The song hails God choosing new leaders, both Deborah, a "mother of Israel," and, she sings, "Most blessed of women be Jael, blessed among tent-dwelling women," recounting her decisive actions against the evil Sisera.

Even for the most biblically literate people, this story is likely not familiar, all perhaps except that last bit. When Elizabeth, pregnant with John the Baptist, is visited by her cousin, Mary, pregnant with Jesus, she famously says, "Blessed are you among women, and blessed is the child you will bear!" Practical Theologian Sarah Jobe writes about the power of this connection between Mary, the mother of Jesus, and Jael, one of the two other women in all of Scripture to be called "blessed" in this way (the other is Judith), and especially its power when read in the context of a women's prison in the United States. She writes, "almost everyone I met who was doing time for murder had killed an intimate partner who had been abusing them for years." It turns out, when a woman kills an intimate partner who is assaulting her, she generally cannot invoke self-defense and is charged with murder, often with long prison sentences. These women, many of them with deeply conflicted feelings of guilt at killing their abuser, found great solace in knowing this story of Jael and her acting against a violent, oppressive man. One could, Jobe writes, see this as a female version of the popular story of David and Goliath, of doing right against great odds, of an underdog fighting against a powerful, violent force and overcoming.[11]

Given my use of the term prophetic as a way to describe the purpose of their work as a band, and the particular and critical perspectives the Roots have regarding race, class, and gender, it makes sense that I would listen to womanist perspectives on biblical stories of prophetic purpose. Womanist theology, as Emilie Townes describes it, "is a form of reflection that places the religious and moral perspectives of Black women at the center of its method." Further, Townes, writes, it centers "the use of an inter-structured analysis employing class, gender, and race" in a critique of oppression, and a vision for ending such harm, "in the lives of African Americans and, extension, the rest of humanity and creation."[12] Biblical scholars like Will Gafney, drawing on a womanist frame, have retold the stories of biblical women in relationship to the stories of women today, opening up the surprising ways they are friends

11. Jobe, "Reading Jael's Story in a Women's Prison."
12. Townes, "Womanist Theology," 1165.

and prophets of God.[13] In lifting up these women's stories, not only is the horror of oppression and marginalization called out for the injustice that it is, but also these women enact a powerful agency in moving towards another world that is possible and that God desires. In embodying these characteristics, Esther, Deborah, and Jael found a purpose within a prophetic tradition, one extending all the way to the present, and encompassing the Roots.

As I said early on in this book, I don't mean hip-hop artists, whether the Roots or otherwise, *are* prophets, but that they (and we) might inhabit a prophetic mode, a way of speaking and living that calls out injustice, and acts to call into being another, more hopeful and just world. One clear way the Roots' work can be seen directly in line with these powerful stories of prophetic biblical women is through their partnership with the street poet Ursula Rucker, who in her contributions to multiple Roots albums directly addresses sexual violence, and calls out the injustices faced and fought against by women from marginalized communities. About the time they joined up with Jimmy Fallon, Trotter puts the band's social critique in this way:

> At this point, in 2008, if you put out a book, a movie, or write a verse, paint a painting, it should have some sort of social value. Art is the polar opposite of the current communication saturation—the elimination of the art of storytelling, the lack of passing traditions on from generation to generation, when two men would just sit down and talk. A return to art that has some meaning, some deeper political value, might be part of the answer.[14]

13. Gafney, *Womanist Midrash*.
14. Scaggs, "Roots of the Roots."

This is as clear a statement of the "purpose" stage the Roots arrived at as one could find: the group's art, their "play" and "passion," should "have some sort of social value." In the next phase of their career, they explore this sense of purpose in the most robust way.

The Purpose of the Roots

It is not surprising to hear Trotter speak of art that matters having a touchstone in meaning, social purpose, and political value. In some sense the Roots, and hip-hop itself, are inheritors of the blues tradition—and the traditions of Black music in America generally—that has always had a sense of purpose linked to the liberation from oppression. While I do not want to reduce a complex weaving to one thread, it is certainly justifiable to say that God's liberation of ancient Israel from slavery to freedom in the Hebrew Bible was and is a foundational story in African American history and culture. As only one expression of this, Harriet Tubman was named Mother Moses for her life-long work as a conductor on the underground railroad, liberating her people from slavery just as Moses had in biblical times. Hip-hop, and prior forms of Black music in America, are, as jazz pianist, composer, and music scholar Vijay Iyer puts it, "revolutionary forms of self-expression. To my ears, these artists possess a certain 'cry,' an incisive, ironic stance with respect to conventional musical forms, practices, and discourses. Often supporting and enriching this approach is a critical sociopolitical outlook, a desire to change the world, that many artists of color cannot help but share."[15] Of course, this awareness on the part of the Roots was present from the beginning, including in the Afrocentricism

15. Iyer, *Memorophilia* liner notes.

and social critique of some of their formative influences like the Native Tongues Collective (De La Soul, especially) and Public Enemy. When it works in this vein, Thompson says when hip-hop is "telling stories about the tearing of society's fabric, about well-intentioned people cast adrift, wasn't it doing the good work that soul music had done before it, and blues before that?"[16]

Still, in some sense this era feels like the Roots maturing into their purpose, into a sense of how to use their steadily growing platform to do that "good work" of telling stories about social ills, and sometimes pointing at how it all might be otherwise. Their first couple of albums after the phenomenal success of *Things Fall Apart* show this searching for where to be now, more than a decade and four albums under their belts. *Phrenology* (2002) turned out to be a success, largely on the strength of the Cody Chesnutt collaboration on the hit single, "The Seed (2.0)." The album overall was unique in that it was in a sense the band bringing out all their toys to play. Thompson called it the first "anti-Roots Roots album," and Rich Nichols, their manager, called it a "messy, circling-the-drain type of affair." Critics loved its expansive character, encompassing genres ranging from hardcore punk to classic R&B and a few socially conscious hip-hop tracks to make it recognizably the Roots. It was, in some sense, them still trying to prove themselves: "We wanted to shatter people's myths, not only about what rap groups could do, but also about what black groups could do," Thompson recalls.[17]

But just as the record was set to come out, their record label was dissolved, and they landed at Interscope. The head of the label at the time, Jimmy Lovine, thought their music sounded dated, and was skeptical. Scott Storch,

16. Thompson, *Mo' Meta Blues*, 168.
17. Thompson, *Mo' Meta Blues*, 194.

the keyboard player for the Roots early on, was now a very successful producer for Interscope, and was set up to help introduce the band to the music of current hitmakers on their label: 50 Cent, Eminem, and others. Lovine pushed the band "to dial back the analytical intelligence at the heart of the record," and make songs following the five second rule: "if a song doesn't grab you within that short span, it's not going to grab you at all." The problem Thompson admits, was that "I didn't know how to make pop music. I only knew how to make smart music."[18] Still, the first track, "Star," number 103 in their unique mode of numbering, is a standout not just on the album but overall across the band's work. Drawing on a catchy sample from "Everybody is a Star," by Sly and the Family Stone, the song is a loving critique of the sometimes foolish bravado of young people that often has devastating consequences: "In Philly, Cincinnati, Los Angeles or Harlem / Kids call themselves killers let they hammers do the talkin' / Don't even know the meaning of life, ain't seen a thing!" The video for the song is a moving depiction of youth in their neighborhoods, trying to make a living, getting by. The song's line honoring their struggle centers the feel of the whole video: "to all my people that are stars, it's our time to shine."[19]

In a way the Roots likely did not anticipate, 2004's *The Tipping Point* was a tipping point for the band. Despite bending to expectations to make a hit record, to "fit in" more with the trends of the moment, the album did worse than their previous two, both critically and commercially. They parted ways with Interscope amidst other personal losses, including the death of J. Dilla, the beloved beat maker they'd worked closely with on recent albums

18. Thompson, *Mo' Meta Blues*, 207.
19. The Roots, "Star."

and related projects with D'Angelo, Common, and others. Picked up by Def Jam, whose then president Jay-Z offered the band permission to be themselves and not worry about commercial success: "Do an album you'll be proud of."[20] The Roots' next album, and those that followed, mark a rebirth for the Roots, one that let them claim their desire to be both musically and artistically creative, as well as being socially and politically relevant.

In a major profile in the *New Yorker*, writer Burkhard Bilger posed a question about why the Roots' albums since *The Tipping Point* have taken such a bleak turn. Thompson's reply is telling. Recalling the years of making 2006's *Game Theory* and 2008's *Rising Down*, there were sometimes more than a dozen murders a week in their hometown of Philadelphia: "It was, like, Whoa, we've got to let the world know about this." The sentiment recalls the view of hip-hop coined by Trotter's MC hero, Chuck D of Public Enemy: "rap is Black America's CNN." While perhaps this quip from Chuck D has gotten more attention than he intended, it is helpful to follow Thompson into his "classroom" mode and hear where he takes this, not in the interview in the *New Yorker*—as Bilger moves on to the tired discussion of the Roots never having a #1 single (correct) or a platinum album (incorrect). In his memoir, Thompson says these more recent records are, in their way, blues records. He goes on to give examples of what he calls, "outward blues," like Blind Willie Johnson's "God Moves Upon the Waters," about the sinking of the *Titanic*, or Minnie Wallace's "The Cockeyed World," about the Italian invasion of Ethiopia in 1935. These songs, and many others, cataloged a world gone wrong, with human hubris and tragedy and violence as the result.

20. Thompson, *Mo' Meta Blues*, 237.

Game Theory, then, was "outward blues." Here, as Trotter did earlier, Thompson offers a sense of the Root's solidifying purpose as artists: "The world had just gone wrong, was continuing to go wrong, whether it was the breached levees in New Orleans or the murder rate in Philadelphia, and we wanted to say so, in no uncertain terms. It was our right as artists but also our responsibility."[21] The album intentionally echoes Public Enemy's *It Takes A Nation of Millions to Hold Us Back* (Def Jam, 1988), an album that has a distinct, political manifesto sensibility. After opening with a tribute to J. Dilla ("Dilltastic Vol Won(derful)"), "False Media" is the first Roots track from the album, numbered 115 in their catalog. Drawing explicitly from the media critique of Public Enemy's "Don't Believe the Hype" even directly lifting a couple of lines for the hook, featuring a Philadelphia artist (and now lawyer) Wadud Ahmad. With a slow, intense percussion-driven

21. Thompson, *Mo' Meta Blues*, 238.

mood, and in the background, an eerie whistle noise that itself evokes Public Enemy, the song has a sober power. The hook, one long verse by Trotter, and the hook, again, repeated until the end. Surely a commentary on police harassment, one phrase states, "keep the bright lights out of our faces/you can't shake it, it ain't no way to swallow the hatred." The album, while serious, also restores the Roots' commitment to hip-hop as a collective art form, as a space to play and explore passion with collaborators, here including nine other mostly Philadelphia-based artists in addition to Ahmad.

Trotter indeed calls *Game Theory* a fundamental shift for the band: "*Game Theory* was the beginning of our albums becoming more conceptual, more focused with regards to subject matter. Even more political. More officially produced. We were able to take out the filler and articulate a vision."[22] Two albums followed quickly on the heels of *Game Theory*, each in their own way carrying forward the "outward blues" idea, but in a sense showing the two sides of the impact of the era born with the election of the first African American president, Barak Obama. On the one hand, a collaboration with fellow Philadelphian John Legend to do an album of uplifting soul remakes celebrating the promise of the Obama era. While recorded in 2008, *Wake Up!* was not released till 2010, and garnered both popular and critical acclaim, eventually winning the Grammy award for best R&B album. The title comes from the inspiring song, "Wake Up, Everybody," originally recorded in 1975 by Harold Melvin & the Blue Notes, with Teddy Pendergrass singing lead vocals. *Rising Down*, released in 2008, took aim at the flip side of Obama's optimism and promise. Businessman Donald Trump started what was eventually termed the "birther" conspiracy claiming

22. Leas, "We've Got A File On You: Black Thought."

Obama was not born in the US and was not, therefore, a legitimate president of the United States. This birther conspiracy, along with many other racially motivated attacks, amounted to a racist backlash against the nation's first Black president, and by association, Black people generally.[23] The album has a thematic consistency, opening and closing with paired tracks, "Rising Down" (129) and "Rising Up" (141). The title of the album, and of these tracks, come from William T. Vollmann's book on the psychology of violence, *Rising Up and Rising Down: Some Thoughts on Violence, Freedom and Urgent Means*.[24] On the first track, "Rising Down," long-time collaborator Karl "Dice Raw" Jenkins takes the hook, setting an ominous tone for the album as a whole: "You don't see that something's wrong/ earth's spinning outta control/everything's for sale, even souls/someone get God on the phone."

It was at this juncture in their story that the fated UCLA meeting between Jimmy Fallon and the Roots took place, leading to a deal to become the house band for Late Night. They reported to the NBC studies in early 2009, running practice shows, and went on the air for their first episode March 2, 2009. While the first show was rocky and got mixed reviews, it, and the shows that followed in those early months, offered hints of the genius match that is Fallon and the Roots. Already on the first episode, examples shine of their playful, yet masterful abilities. On that first episode, they debut a bit called "Slow Jamming the News." It was the last news item in Fallon's opening monologue, amounts to slowing down the news story with Fallon telling the main story, and Trotter and the Roots doing a sexy R&B vibe as back-up. With this mode, most any news

---

23. "Barack Obama citizenship conspiracy theories."
24. NPR Staff, "The Roots: Rising Up with Rising Down."

story can seem to be a little suggestive, even a story—in this example—about Nancy Pelosi in congress.

Then, Fallon, who is very musically talented, broke into an impression with Justin Timberlake, the second guest of the night. As guests walk out, the Roots play a "walk-on" which is a snippet from a song, chosen because of its connection to the guest. In this case, they played the Bee Gees' "Nights on Broadway" as that was the basis of the spoof song Timberlake and Fallon used for a skit on *Saturday Night Live* called, "The Barry Gibbs Talk Show," with Fallon as Barry Gibbs, and Timberlake as his brother, Robin. As Timberlake sat down, laughing, he pointed to the Roots, and broke into the song again, imitating the Bee Gees' falsetto, with Fallon and the Roots seamlessly joining in. Other bits with the Roots followed, including "Freestyling with the Roots," where Jimmy interviews an audience member and then Trotter and the Roots make a song of it. Were it to just be a beat and freestyle rap based on the audience member's information, that'd be easy, but Fallon also names the music genre for the song: "not just hip hop, but as surf music, or heavy metal, or country."[25] And, famously, in summer 2012, they began doing feature songs with musical guests using only children's instruments, beginning with pop sensation Carly Rae Jepson's hit song, "Call Me Maybe." The video quickly became a viral sensation that now has 32 million views on YouTube. These hilarious classroom instrument covers continue on *The Tonight Show*, and as Questlove puts it, "let us bring out our inner-13-year-old."[26]

These playful bits show that as people find their purpose "in prime time" so to speak, it does not mean that play and passion go away, but rather that they are

25. Thompson, *Mo' Meta Blues*, 248.

26. Thompson, Interview on Fuse.

channeled, and in a way, mature. Sometimes, such lessons in moderating play and passion to a larger platform, to a more mature sense of purpose, come at the cost of very painful circumstances. A major example for the Roots occurred when conservative Minnesota congresswoman Michelle Bachmann, then running for president, made an appearance on the show late in 2011. Thompson notes that she "had been offending people left and right with her comments about gay rights and Muslims in America, and she seemed to have a casual relationship to the truth." He struck out to find a walk-on for the show "about politics and evasion and untruth."[27] He settled on Fishbone's "Lyin' Ass Bitch," a fun ska song from their 1985 debut album, and it went off without a hitch.

**Michelle Bachmann during the infamous
"Lyin' Ass Bitch" walk-on for a 2012 episode of *Late Night*.**

27. Thompson, *Mo' Meta Blues*, 261.

Feeling smug, and even righteous, thinking he "had done something historic, something political," he copped to the use of the song on Twitter. The story went viral, and by the next day, conservative media were calling for Fallon and the Roots' heads. Soon, the backlash expanded to women offended by the use of "bitch" as derogatory. After a tense meeting, Jimmy Fallon offered an apology on Twitter, laying blame directly at Thompson's feet where, he readily admits, it belonged. However, a day later, on Tuesday night, Bachman made a serious factual blunder in a presidential primary debate, setting her staff on another focus, and that weekend's Thanksgiving break cooled things off. However, Thompson raises another reason the storm passed without further harm to the Roots. Through a connection at Fox News, he learned they had combed through every Roots album looking for offensive lyrics—something violent, something misogynistic—and came up empty. Wryly, Thompson notes that "the politically correct, mindful hip-hop that we had been practicing from the beginning—the same thing that had keep us off the chart or kept our posters off the walls of teenagers' bedrooms—had worked to our advantage."[28]

The band were unsure what creativity would be left over after the grind of a five-day-a-week day job as a house band for Jimmy Fallon—first on *Late Night*, and then *The Tonight Show*. Yet in some ways, the first album after starting on *Late Night*, 2010's *How I Got Over*, channels a moment of maturity for the band. Thompson calls it a "spiritual awakening." While I've already detailed some significant religious influences on Thompson and Trotter in the introduction, as they moved into their 40s, they were most sure what they couldn't be anymore. In middle

28. Thompson, *Mo' Meta Blues*, 264.

age, there is no "throw your hands in the air, wave 'em like you don't care." But what should they be? The album title they chose tells part of the story.[29]

How I Got Over, the Roots' ninth studio album, draws its album title from a well-known and beloved Gospel hymn written by Clara Ward in 1951 and made famous by Mahalia Jackson. About the same time, on the joint album titled *Wake Up!* with fellow Philadelphia recording artist John Legend, Trotter was rhyming about listening to Mahalia on Sundays at his grandmother's house. The song "How I Got Over" has spiritual, but also social justice echoes for African Americans. It is about "getting over" in the double sense of heavenly and this-worldly salvation. Jackson performed the song at the 1963 March on Washington just before Dr. Martin Luther King Jr. took the podium for his historic "I Have a Dream" speech. The Roots have repeatedly said their album titles are a commentary on three levels: what is happening with the Roots, with hip-hop, and with the world.[30] With the Roots, the house band gig with Jimmy Fallon let the band exhale, not tour 330 days of 365 days per year to make their bread and butter, and the experience was remarkably creative. In that sense they "got over" to the success they'd always hoped for, but without telling the story in a pollyannaish way. It takes grit.

On the level of hip-hop and on the level of the world, the album reflects their long-time focus on the plight of African Americans, with a particular hopefulness given the 2008 election of President Barak Obama. Yet here, too, they are not brushing aside the difficulties which still exist. The centerpiece of the album, the searching collaboration

29. Thompson, *Mo' Meta Blues*, 254.
30. Thompson, *Mo' Meta Blues*, 202.

with Monsters of Folk for a cover of their song "Dear God (Sincerely M.O.F.)," came about through a guest appearance on *Late Night*. The Roots backed them for the performance, and when they sang it in rehearsal, Thompson recalls, "it just blew me away. . . I thought it was the best gospel song I had heard in what seemed like forever, but it also sounded like an ego song that was crying out for a Ghostface Killah rhyme." He immediately approached Jim James of My Morning Jacket, one of four members in the supergroup Monsters Of Folk (also includes Conor Oberst, Mike Mogis, and M. Ward), to ask if they could record the song.

The song begins hauntingly with James singing, "Dear God / I'm trying hard to reach you / Dear God / I see your face in all I do / Sometimes it's so hard to believe in / But God, I know you have your reasons." Later, the song turns to a lament, a complaint against God. The singer plaintively asks, "But if your love's still around / Why do we suffer?" Thompson felt it wasn't so much questioning the existence of God. Instead, he draws on the logic of the lament tradition, where questions to God are offered on the basis of a relationship with God, with a sharp expectation that because of who God is, things ought to be different. Thompson puts it this way: "It was more about social justice, and how any divine being with an interest in his human creation would allow certain circumstances to persist. It reminded me of what KRS-One said on his album Edutainment twenty years before: 'If the Christians really heard Christ / The black man never would've lived this life.'"[31]

Trotter picked up on this mood in his rhymes, interpolated with the basic frame of the Monsters of Folk

31. Thompson, *Mo' Meta Blues*, 255.

song, which in the end they titled "Dear God 2.0." Trotter's first verse rhymes through a catalog of the troubles of the world, from "Acid rain, earthquakes, hurricane, tsunamis / terrorists, crime sprees, assaults and robberies" to "Air quality so foul, I gotta try to breathe / Endangered species, and we're running out of trees." But in his second verse digs into more personal territory: "They send my daddy to you in a barrage of bullets / Why is the world ugly when you made it in your image?" In the process of developing this one song, Thompson says, a mood spread to the whole album. It was a way to mature as a band, "offering a dig-nified path into middle age" for themselves and for their fans.[32]

32. Thompson, *Mo' Meta Blues*, 255.

5

Conclusion: "Who Lives, Who Dies, Who Tells Your Story?"

Ahmir "Questlove" Thompson has the humorous habit of saying, when describing big decisions in the unfolding story of the Roots, "I couldn't see our Wikipedia page ending that way." This book's conclusion is in no way intended to say how the Wikipedia page ends either. The career of the Roots, and of its individual members, is still very much active and unfolding. My desire here is much more modest than offering a summative evaluation of the Roots' journey through play and passion to finding their purpose. Instead, I can offer a final story from their career, one that offers a window into how their platform on *The Tonight Show* offers them specific opportunities to act on their purpose. If you recall, the Roots aim to engage three levels of meaning in choosing an album name: their personal lives, the world of hip-hop, and, as Nina Simone put it in describing the duty of the artist, "to reflect the times." Finding themselves with a steady gig on a major international platform like

The Tonight Show lets them explore their purpose in highly significant ways, as in, for example, the remarkable story of the landmark musical Hamilton and their collaboration with its creator, Lin-Manuel Miranda.

The musical began when Miranda picked up Ron Chernow's tome *Alexander Hamilton* for a vacation read, and quickly came to the surprising conclusion that Hamilton's story was a hip-hop story. He hatched the idea of a mixtape telling the story. In 2009, an invitation to a White House Evening of Poetry, Music, and the Spoken Word in hand, Miranda wowed a skeptical President Obama and his guests with the eventual opening song of the musical: "How does a bastard, orphan, son of a whore and a Scotsman, dropped in the middle of a forgotten spot in the Caribbean by providence impoverished in squalor, grow up to be a hero and a scholar?" Fast forward to early 2015 and *Hamilton: The Musical* was in rehearsals for its off-Broadway premier at The Public Theater in New York. Tariq "Black Thought" Trotter recalls being "part of the first musicians that Lin invited to check the play out," and it was, he says, "like an instant partnership, instant mutual admiration."[1] Although big fans of Miranda's previous Broadway hit musical, *In the Heights*, they had not met before. It turns out Miranda, a big hip-hop fan, had loved the Roots since seeing them play on campus during his college days at Wesleyan.

The Roots co-founders—both Thompson and Trotter—loved *Hamilton* immediately. Thompson, however, describes being "set back a step" upon seeing it for the first time. Being the self-described "pop-culture obsessive" both as a creator and consumer, he wanted to make sense of what exactly Miranda had pulled off—to his mind something never before achieved—or, for that matter, imagined. For starters, Thompson says, the play pulls off a radical upending of the history run by white people, now "in Hamilton, played by Latino or African American performers, without any explanation." Part of the power, in fact, is its lack of explanation. In a conversation with Miranda, Thompson humorously quips that his first time at the show, "For me, it wasn't until the third time the king came out when I was like, "Wait a second . . . " and Miranda retorts, "He's the only white guy!" Yet the reason Thompson thinks the show "is blowing people's wigs back" is that this show is the "first real synthesis of two great institutions: the Broadway musical and hip-hop." He further specifies the accomplishment is not just "a hip-hop musical or a stage presentation of hip-hop; its organically and genuinely both things at once . . . "[2]

The cultural moment of the Roots move to *The Tonight Show* and the initial staging of Hamilton at the Public Theater plays into the significance of the collaboration and its social impact. During these same years, a major social

1. Rys, "Roots Black Thought on Lin-Manuel Miranda."
2. Thompson, Questlove on 'Hamilton' and Hip-Hop."

movement arose in response to the shootings of young black men by police. The murders of Trayvon Martin in Florida and Michael Brown in Missouri sparked both the #BlackLivesMatter movement and a new national conversation now coming to fruition in the current moment of uprising and demand for justice in 2020. All along, the Roots found personal and professional means to lend support to efforts for racial justice. A marker of the social shifts over this period with regard to support for protests against police brutality are dramatically displayed in the growth of public opinion in support of the #BlackLives-Matter movement. It ought to be said that cries against police brutality echo in the voices of hip-hop artists from its very beginning in the 1970s. And my wager is that the combined impact of the Roots on *The Tonight Show* and *Hamilton* on Broadway contributed to the current cultural tipping point. This impact is likely especially powerful for white people who are majority audiences for these two cultural institutions. As is the case with complex social change, causality is not simple to show, but the power of their contribution is undeniable.

⟿

With the combination of the security and creative diversity of their *Tonight Show* position and inspiration from high profile collaborations like Hamilton, it is no surprise that their most recent two albums, *Undun* (2011) followed by . . . *And Then You Shoot Your Cousin* (. . . *ATYSYC*, 2014), are their most creative risks yet. The Roots had long shown interest in concept albums in hip-hop, having thrown props at Prince Paul for his groundbreaking work on De La Soul's 1991 album *De La Soul Is Dead*, as well as his own 1999 concept album *A Prince Among Thieves*, a story of a young hustler and wannabe rapper named Tariq. The album begins at the end of the story, as EMT's attend to the wounded Tariq.

Undun and . . . *ATYSYC* are, like Prince Paul's work, conceptual albums that tell stories of urban suffering and violence. *Undun* begins much the same *A Prince Among Thieves*, with the death of the main character, in this case, a young man named Redford Stevens. The album runs in reverse-chronological order starting from the track "Dun" featuring the haunting sound of a beeping flatline. *Undun's* tragic narrative creates a powerfully impacting album. Three years later, as Thompson published a six-part series of essays on how "Hip-Hop Failed Black America," the Roots released . . . *ATYSYC*, the most haunting and chal- lenging album to date. It is the work of mature artists who, having passed all their tests, are now teaching the class.

In his first article, "When the People Cheer: How Hip-Hop Failed Black America," a title shared by the third track on . . . *ATYSYC*, Thompson laments that hip-hop has both "taken over black music" and the culture as a whole, losing its soul in the process. He asks, "what if hip-hop, which was once a form of upstart black-folk music, came to dominate the modern world?" This is not, it should be said, a self-critique of their achieving the platform of *The Tonight Show*, or, for that matter, the success of the first hip-hop Broadway musical. Rather, as in their earlier song "What They Do" from 1996's *Illadelph Halflife*, Thompson is hammering the critique of hip-hop selling its soul for an almighty dollar. As I discuss in chapter 3 above, that song, and especially its accompanying video, were a hilari- ous parody of Chris "Biggie" Wallace's single "One More Chance" from his album of the same year, *Born to Die*. The critique of hip-hop losing its roots as a new generation's "upstart black-folk music," lies in hip-hop artists becoming "shallowly materialistic or who permit themselves to be reduced to caricature."

The core of Thompson's argument is not to say hip-hop should be less brash, or that artists should not desire success and all it brings. To make his point, he pulls together three disparate ideas and draws a triangle to show the intersecting ideas. The first is from sixteenth-century reformer John Bradford, who coined the phrase, "There, but by the grace of God go I, on luck and providence." The second is from Albert Einstein about unintended impact and concern for community. And the third is from rapper Ice Cube about aspirations and appetite for success. Hip-hop's sweet spot lies, Thompson argues, inside the triangle where people reflect on their own good fortune, recognize they're connected to others and grapple with their own aspirations in relation to the needs of one's community. It is in a sense saying, when you make the big time, don't forget where you came from. Hip-hop, Thompson notes, has always been about material things. In part that is true of American celebrity culture generally, but it has a particular logic for hip-hop. "Hip-hop is about having things to prove you're not a have-not; it works against the notion that you might have so little economic control that you would simply disappear."

Thompson turns to an extended example to make the case about what's happened to hip-hop, showing that what signifies being among the "haves" has shifted due to the transformation of the art form, or perhaps more to his point, the malformation of the art form. Thirty years ago, when the Roots were just getting started as a group, the top artists in the genre were Run-DMC. One of their biggest hits was a song called, "My Adidas," after the shoes that were both part of their distinctive look, and something totally relatable to (and affordable for) their average listener. Thompson puts it this way, saying "they sold a cool that was accessible to their fans." Now with record companies increasingly only willing to invest in "sure-bet" mega-artists, and with the outsized rewards they reap, the "haves" are "on the opposite side of the planet, ethically and socially, from 'My Adidas.'" By way of example, he references Jay Z's song "Picasso Baby," from his 2013 album *Magna Carta . . . Holy Grail.* The song begins, "I just want a Picasso, in my casa, No, my castle" and before long he's described himself as "the new Jean Michel, surrounded by Warhols," a reference to the late New York City-based artists, Jean-Michel Basquiat, whose paintings are among the most expensive in the art world. While "My Adidas" is about ordinary items, affordable to their fans, hip-hop has gone to a place now where the references are "unattainable luxury, fantasy acquisitions."

In further installments, Thompson argues that commercialization of hip-hop leads to a loss of "black cool," ironically coming to mirror the slick and predictable production values of the genre it originally defined itself against: disco. Hip-hop, as he sees it, has become all about product, and moving product, rather than a process connected to the struggles of the Black community. Thompson quotes Harlem Renaissance scholar Charles S. Johnson arguing that the "arts . . . could be a site of resistance." "In its simplest terms," Thompson writes, "art humanizes." What Black American music does, in terms of resistance, he argues, is force the dominant culture to "see black musicians as virtuosos with complex ideas and powerful (and recognizable) emotions. How are you going to treat someone as less than human, in a way, once they've been so deeply human in full view?"[3] Ultimately, Questlove argues, "art . . . should be about humanity, and culture should, in some way, be a tool for fighting adversity." That mainstream hip-hop has on the whole abandoned such lofty aims for a singular focus on the bottom line is a provocation that can't be allowed to stand. And their album, . . . *And Then You Shoot Your Cousin*, is their most sophisticated effort to date to push back at the hip-hop world, to make the case, again, for the arts as a site of resistance, for art that humanizes.

Tariq Trotter, in an interview at the time of the . . . *ATYSYC*'s release, compared it to *Undun,* which takes on the goal of hip-hop as a humanizing art form by telling the story of one young man. "His tragic death served as a metaphor for the plight of urban youth in America." . . . *ATYSYC* attempts the same goal by telling many stories. "We create quite a few different characters on this record," Trotter says. "We as artists, musicians, Philadelphians, New Yorkers, we as black men, we're familiar with very many of these characters, and we kind of introduce them to the rest of the world in a manner that makes them more easily understood."[4] The Roots' album covers often offer social and political commentary on the subject of the album, and this case is no different. Embodying the larger goals for the concept album, they chose Romare Bearden's 1964 collage titled, "Pittsburgh Memory," that depicts two Black men staring directly out of the frame at the viewer, as if saying, "We're here, do you see us?" A founding member of the Harlem-based civil rights artists collective, The

---

3. Thompson, "Questlove: Does Black Culture Need to Care About What Happens to Hip-Hop?"

4. Rys, "Roots' New Project will be a Concept Album."

Spiral, Bearden's life and art embody well Thompson's argument about the arts being as site of resistance.[5]

Yet, upon release, the album met with quizzical faces and even dismissal as containing "too much to unpack."[6] Even Trotter, after trying to explain the concepts behind the album, reacted defensively to the hip-hop magazine *XXL:* "I don't know if that makes any sense." The title is lifted from KRS-One's song "Step Into A World": "MCs more worried about their financial backin'/ Steady packin' a gat as if something's gonna happen/ But it doesn't, they wind up shootin' they cousin, they buggin'." This quote used as the title builds in the satire and lament of pointless

5. Brown, "Black History Art: Romare Bearden."
6. Madden, "Roots— . . . And Then You Shoot Your Cousin."

violence and suffering in contemporary urban life, a point
the album makes to challenge their audience and hip-hop
more generally. Some took their invitation to listen in and
learn, and found the experience richly rewarding. The fact
is, like hip-hop more broadly, many of the reviewers on
music websites are white men overly influenced by the
commercial, stereotyped hip-hop of exactly the sort the
Roots are take aim at with this album. Typical of this kind
of review, white Milwaukee-based music writer Evan Rytlewski writes that the Roots have all but given up on a mass
appeal. "The band's elusive 11th studio album," he writes
in summary, is "so fragmented that when it breaks for a
noise collage from French experimental composer Michel
Chion halfway through, it hardly feels like a disruption."[7]

One of the best reviews I read was by the music writer,
Lucas Garrison, whose title would likely make Thompson
break out in his beautiful smile so familiar to fans of *The
Tonight Show*. Garrison titled his review, "The Roots' ' . . .
And Then You Shoot Your Cousin' Album Made Me a Better Music Fan."[8] He begins by citing another article on the
DJBooth website, Yoh Phillips's "Want Better Hip-Hop? Be
a Better Fan," that influenced and challenged him. Phillips
quotes the great American poet Walt Whitman who once
said, "To have great poets, there must be great audiences."[9]
Garrison, in his review, slowly listens to and learns from
. . . ATYSYC, in the process showing how it made him a
better hip-hop listener. It turns out Garrison had been
reading Thompson's six-essay collection, "How Hip-Hop
Failed Black America," on vulture.com, and in summary

7. Rytlewski, "The Roots lay on the satire with the arty . . . *And
Then You Shoot Your Cousin*."

8. Garrison, "The Roots' ' . . . And Then You Shoot Your Cousin'
Album Made Me A Better Music Fan."

9. Phillips, "What Better Hip-Hop? Be A Better Fan."

argues for the album as "having a purpose, a well-thought-out, well-crafted mission."[10]

Even as careful a listener as Garrison, however, admits being perplexed by track 7 (track 177 in the Roots catalog), the snippet of the French experimental musician Michel Chion titled "Dies Irae." Garrison writes, "I can find something enjoyable on all but 'Dies Irae' (no idea what that was)." I think, however, it might be the key to the album's form as a piece of art. On the album as a whole, the Roots play with the standard hip-hop pattern of sampling. The standard form of sampling takes a snippet of another song, and plays it on repeat behind the rhyming of the MC, a practice that developed with the Bronx hip-hop pioneer DJ Kool Herc in order to indefinitely stretch out the rhythmic "break" in songs. Here, however, in addition to some classic sampling (Blackrock's 1972 soul tune, "Yeah Yeah" used for Black Rock), the band has placed samples as distinct, standalone tracks interspersed through the album. The opening track is Nina Simone's "Theme from the Middle of the Night," from the 1959 movie of the same name, while track 4 is Mary Lou Williams's "The Devil" from her groundbreaking 1964 album, *Black Christ of the Andes*. Each of these is interesting in their own right, playing to the overall theme of the album. But just in the middle of the album (track 7 out of 11 on the album), the third sample track is Chion's "Dies Irae" from his 1978 release *Requiem*.

The requiem, a classical form of sung masses based on the funeral mass, has been used by the most famous of composers in the West: Duruflé, Mozart, Verdi, and more. Of course, in the twentieth century, Britten used the form

10. Garrison, "The Roots' ' . . . And Then You Shoot Your Cousin' Album Made Me A Better Music Fan."

for his haunting "War Requiem," an example of using the form not only as a funeral mass but also as social critique. Slipped between the historic texts of the church, Britten inserts poetry regarding the horrors of war from Wilfred Owen who himself was killed in action in November of 1918 towards the end of World War I. The "*Dies Irae*," the fifth part of the classic structure of the requiem mass, is a form of the sequence, a liturgical poem used before the reading of the Gospel. With roots in early medieval Europe, the "*Dies Irae*" (literally "the day of wrath) describes the Last Judgment when a trumpet sounds and summons all souls before God, those who are saved being led into heaven, and the damned being cast into eternal flames.

In Michel Chion's words, the *Requiem*—and the "*Dies Irae*" in particular—"was composed whilst thinking about the troubled minority of the living, rather than the silent majority of the dead."[11] Tom Schulte, writing a review for AllMusic.com, gets the sense of the piece exactly: "While such classic requiems glorify the suggestion of eternal life suggested by the religious interpretation of death, Chion's work probes the existential panic of those living under the threat of death. A dark, kaleidoscope collage of cruel whispers, snippets of choral works, and eerie, segmented sacred string music promote a feeling of uneasiness and abandonment."[12] This existential dread evoked the "*Dies Irae*," and the *Requiem* as a whole, describes exactly what the Roots aim at in their portraits of urban hopelessness..

. . . *ATYSYC* opens with the soulful and sorrowful Nina Simone singing the title track from the 1959 movie, *Theme from the Middle of the Night*: "Only the lonely love, only the sad of soul, Wake and begin their day in the middle

11. Chion, "Requiem."
12. Schulte, "Review of Michael Chion, Requiem."

of the night." This song sets the stage for an album "sad of soul." The first Roots' track, and first single released from the album, "Never," features the Icelandic, now Philadelphian, singer Patty Crash. Its musical feel and lyrics allow the band set their own take on "the sad of soul." The album was recorded with the Metropolis Ensemble for added orchestral support, and the Howard Roberts Choral Group for added vocals, both under the direction of Andrew Cyr, conductor.[13] Although they are often called "The Legendary Roots Crew" as a result of being a live band with many artistic collaborators, these orchestral and choral collaborations take this album into new musical territory.

When the Roots traded their house band status for guest musicians on *The Tonight Show* with Jimmy Fallon in celebration of the album's release, it was to perform "Never" with the full orchestra and chorale on stage.[14] The song begins with two snare drum pops from Thompson, sounding like shots of a gun. The choir softly begins singing a slow, mournful, "agnus, agnus" before the piano comes in mirroring the agnus, and then layered over the piano, drums and choir, Patty Crash comes in with the hook: "Sweet dreams, close your eyes/Say goodbye to my memory." This beginning is another subtle bow to the Requiem and its "*Agnus Dei, qui tolls piccata mundi: dona eis requiem.*" Translated, this means "Lamb of God, who takes away the sins of the world, grant them rest." In a sense, the whole album is about how hard that peace is to find, at least on this side of death. In Trotter's verse for "Never," he rhymes a series of masterful depictions of despair: "No family ties nigga, no laces / Less than a full deck nigga, no

13. Metropolis Ensemble, "The Roots' And Then You Shoot Your Cousin."

14. The Roots, "Tonight Show Performance of 'Never.'"

aces / Waitin' on Superman, losing all patience / Gettin' wasted on an everyday basis / I'm stuck here, can't take a vacation / So fuck it, this shit is damnation." The outro, sung by Patty Crash, puts an exclamation point on the despair: "I woke up with a tear drop / All I know, it's all I know."

From this beginning, the album's tracks—and Trotter, along with two other MCs who are longtime collaborators—tell different stories. Yet the characters all live variations on the theme of hopelessness and suffering. In his verse for "Black Rock," Karl "Dice Raw" Jenkins depicts the hardship of food insecurity and the temptations of escape through available means—a 40-ounce bottle of malt liquor and a quarter ounce of marijuana: "Yo, what's for breakfast? Same as yesterday / Oh, that's right, cheeseburger and a 40 ounce / Then what's for dinner? Nothing, nigga / But last night I had dreams of a porterhouse /For real, for real, I feel like cattle in a slaughterhouse / but fuck that, roll one up, yo, here's a quarter ounce." Then in the track "Understand," just before the "*Dies Irae*," Gregory "Greg Porn" Spearman puts the theme of divine judgment, the subject of the *Dies Irae* as the day of wrath, front and center in the song's hook "People ask for God, 'till the day he comes / See God's face, turn around and run." Religious themes continue in his verse, as well: "Holy, sugar, honey ice tea / I guess that's a prayer for a player like me . . . " Using the first letters of each word shows that the character's actual prayer is "Holy shit." Then in track 8 (178, in the Roots' catalog listing), directly after the "*Dies Irae*," Mercedes Martinez, one half of the Philadelphia-based duo The Jazzyfatnastees, and widow of the Root's manager Richard Nichols, who was instrumental in the album, and died just after its release, delivers a haunting, yet simple piano and vocal track. It begins, "I hear somebody screaming / Again, bracing for a fall / Close my eyes, but I never wonder / I have seen it all." Then, mid-song, the Metropolis Ensemble enters with a kind of musical chaos evoking the feeling of falling. Throughout the album, inclusive of the samples, the music tells the story just as much as the lyrics.

There is a world-weariness in many of the characters sketched here, and perhaps nowhere more ominously than the second to last track, the first of a final pair of tracks featuring soul singer Raheem DeVaughn. "The Unraveling" is the unfolding of a first-person account of a dying soul, as DeVaughn sings in the hook, "And I die here within . . . A man with no future." In Trotter's verse, he references the famous scene in the Bible where Jesus is crucified between two thieves: "What did the thief say unto the hanging man? / 'Here come the hounds, lay your burdens down in advance.'" The loss of what feels like an inconsequential life finds form later in his rhyme, "Came from nowhere, disappear just as fast / A life out of balance, a touch out of grasp / A time traveler headed to a night catches us / The final stop on the line for all passengers." Yet, just as in the Requiem Mass, the dread of death and judgment is not the final word, and so here, too, the seeming meaninglessness signaled from the title's reference to the accidental shooting of one's cousin through the hopelessness of the many characters in the tracks is not left without an answer.

That answer comes, at least in a gesture, via second of this pair of tracks with DeVaughn, the closing track of the album, written with Ray Angry, a collaborator on both *Undun* as well as . . . *ATYSYC*. Similar to the concluding piece of the Requiem Mass, "*In Paradisum*," that focuses, as the title suggests, on finding eternal rest in paradise, the final track of . . . *ATYSYC* is an upbeat feel to match its title: "Tomorrow." DeVaughn sings in the hook, "Cause everybody needs an angel / And everybody needs a smile

/ and everybody has an angle / And everybody wants to-morrow right now." The song reads like a positive thinking manual with such lines saying happiness will never find you till you find yourself, and that it is free to be your-self. Yet it is not a self-serving song in the end, but, more along the lines of Thompson's writing on "How Hip-Hop Failed Black America," that focused on care for self as a way to care for community. The second verse ends with DeVaughn singing, "It costs nothing / It costs nothing to help sometimes," and then repeating in the outro, "And everybody wants tomorrow right now." The final time through the hook ends a full 90 seconds from the end of the song. What has been simple instrumentation—percus-sive drums and piano with vocals— now flows into a lush pop melody that grooves along, resolving into the piano player banging chords all the way up the keyboard, seem-ingly ending the song by storming the gates of paradise musically.

In December of 2019, I took the train downtown and over to Brooklyn, heading to a pop-up event featuring Tariq "Black Thought" Trotter. The evening was sponsored by Okayplayer, a progressive music and culture site founded in 1998 by the Roots' Amir "Questlove" Thompson and Angela "Stress" Nissel. They partnered with SCENE, a community that connects creatives of color through two core questions: "When was the first time you felt seen in your industry?" and "When was the first time you saw yourself?" The warehouse space was painted bright white, with SCENE's two orienting questions written on the wall. As we entered the room, attendees were offered plain cards and sharpie markers to write and post our own answers on the wall. About twenty minutes early, there were no available seats and I took my place against the wall in the rear of the space. Soon introductions began, and SCENE founder Jasmine Martin emerged to introduce and then interview Trotter. A couple of remarkable, vulnerable, and interrelated statements struck me. First, in a humbling admission, Trotter says he's sober, clean, for the first time in decades. He's feeling more focus, more creative energy, than he has for years. Second, in an unsurprising admission, Trotter says doing *The Tonight Show* has become a kind of good boredom. After years of doing the show day after day, they have the rhythm down, and his work on Jimmy Fallon acts as a launching pad to explore lots of other creative outlets including a series of powerful solo albums with the title "Streams of Thought," as well as activist work like the GrassROOTS Community Foundation whose mission is "building a world where all girls can grow up to be healthy women."[15] The rapt audience hangs on the conversation as he turns to encourage young artists of color in the room.

15. Trotter founded GrassROOTS Community Foundation with

As the conversation wrapped up, I joined the crowd spilling out into the dark streets of Brooklyn, and popped in my Airpods, pulling up Trotter's *Streams of Thought, Vol. 1*, released in 2018. I smiled thinking of his viral, jaw-dropping freestyle nearly 10 minutes long performed in late 2017 on Funkmaster Flex's show on Hot 97.1 FM in New York City. The fact that it sparked the attention it did—more than a million YouTube views in 24 hours, and to date nearly 12 million, helped renew claims he is the best MC working today.[16] Of course, I think, the Roots are the *Tonight Show* band because they can play with anyone, can play any style, can cover any tune in any genre. Yet, stripped to their simplest form, the Roots are Thompson making beats and Trotter making rhymes. And in a sense, I think, Trotter is upholding the Roots' street credibility in the hip-hop world and using his position to teach a class by example on the how-to's of classic hip-hop lyricism. Remarking on hip-hop today, Trotter told *Rolling Stone*, "We're at a point in history where lyricism almost comes last in very many regards." Admitting that there are "artists who make those sorts of beats, and record those sorts of lyrics, and performances, and carry that same cadence." "But," Trotter explains, "they don't necessarily have the same sort of platform."[17] Echoing Nina Simone's views from a generation before, Trotter names the political responsibility of his platform: "As an artist, I do share a certain level of responsibility to inform people who look to artists for information. I don't feel it's my job to be a politician—I feel like I'm political by choice and I make

Dr. Janice Johnson Dias who serves as its President. See https://grass-rootscommunityfoundation.org/.

16. Trotter, Freestyle at HOT 97 with Funk Flex.

17. Reeves, "Roots' Black Thought on How He Spit a Nearly 10-Minute Viral Freestyle."

104

the socio-political commentary in my music by choice. But whether I choose to or not because I'm an artist and because I have this platform and because I have this access to so many eyes and ears and minds, there's a certain level of responsibility to speak the truth, and to speak truth to power."[18]

He displays such lyricism—and his broader commitment to speak truth to power—on the latest EP in the series: *Streams of Thought, Volume 3: Cain & Able*, released in mid-October 2020. The title carries a clever double meaning, at once political and personal. One level is classic hip-hop: Trotter, one of the best rappers ever to pick up the mic, is "able" and the producer with whom he partners on this effort, Deleno "Sean C" Matthews, is "Cain." But the more obvious—and more political—meaning of the title comes from the story of Cain and Abel, the two sons of Adam and Eve in the Bible. This is the story of the first murder, the beginning of human violence. When God asks Cain where his brother is, knowing full well he has killed him, Cain says, "Am I my brother's keeper?"[19] It poses a fundamental, prophetic question about the kind of society we live in. And given the ubiquity of the police killings of unarmed black men, while bearing the motto "To Serve and Protect," the title has even more bite.

The opening track from *Cain & Able* sets a clear trajectory for the EP as a whole. Titled, "I'm Not Crazy (First Contact)," the track embodies what Matthews describes as a concept album on oppression: "It goes through everything, from relationships to the indigenous plight to what Blacks are going through . . . we are this planet of all these different people, and oppressed people are everywhere, in

---

18. Uitti, "Black Thought Wants to Speak Truth to Power."
19. Gen 4:1–13.

every country, and most of them are of color." The focus on Native concerns came out of their work with Portland-based indie rockers Portugal. The Man who, because of their Alaska roots, have been drawn to activism on Native causes throughout their career. The track opens with repetition of a simple D-G sequence of two notes on the piano, and the drums, dancing bells and chanting from Native peoples accompanying the voice of Dakota author and activist John Trudell from a speech critiquing Columbus Day. "So, when Columbus got here, he got off the boat and said to the first people he saw: 'Who are you?' And the first people he saw said, 'We're human beings.'"

Black Thought's rhymes weave back and forth with pieces of Trudell's speech ending with "Anyway, when Columbus got here, And he didn't know what it meant to be a human being." This is the sentiment of the fundamental dehumanization at the core of our society's Native genocide and hundreds of years of slavery for Africans. In the outro for the track, we hear a recording from Matthews in 2019 when he happened upon a gang of police officers surrounding and kneeling on top of a Black man on New York City's Upper West Side. The voices of Matthews, filming the episode on his phone, and the cops trying to push him away, give way to Stokely Carmichael's words at the Free Huey Rally of 1968: "Love, patience, brotherhood, and unity. We try and we try and we try. If they become a threat." Static breaks in covering over the end of what Carmichael actually said in his speech: "we off them." The static transitions to the start of the second track, "State Prisoner," where we hear Carmichael continue from the same 1968 speech saying "We need each other, we have to have each other for our survival." The album's bookend, "I'm Not Crazy (Outro)" begins with Trotter rhyming, "A

CONCLUSION

man called Portugal got with the oracle / we move from
metaphorical to historical," cleverly referencing the partnership between Portugal. The Man, and himself as the ancient Greek oracle who acted as a medium through whom
prophecy was sought. Then, ending where the album
began, John Trudell says, "So, when, when we, when we
introduced ourselves to the Europeans as human beings,
they just didn't get it." "Didn't get it" then echoes over and
over for the final 10 seconds.

The truth is, the whole Roots crew benefit from both
the platform and the security and the regularity of *The
Tonight Show*. Their collective creativity and individual
pursuits are blossoming, from the three (thus far) *Streams
of Thought* albums from Trotter, Thompson's writing (most
recently, *Music is History*), DJing, new film ventures including the hit films *Soul*, and *The Summer of Soul*, as well
as inventing partnerships to put vegan Philly cheese steak
sandwiches in sports arenas nationwide, to guitarist Kirk
Douglass releasing a stellar solo album, *Turbulent Times*,
under the name Hundred Watt Heart, enlisting Roots'
bassist Mark Kelley on the project, to pianist James Poyser's
gigging around New York City with his jazz quartet, and a
forthcoming Roots' album called *Endgame* for which the
band have reportedly recorded a stunning 263 new songs.
They are also using their platform for engagement on public issues, for example Trotter lending his voice to the *45lies
Project* calling out President Donald Trump or Thompson
working his instagram account to get out the vote in Philadelphia (which proved to be crucial—as Pennsylvania put
Joseph R. Biden Jr. over the top in the 2020 presidential
race). Whether it be their creative work on these many
projects or their engagement in public issues, the Roots
are living out their prophetic purpose, seeking to build a
better, more joyful, and more equitable world.

∽

One final move brings us full circle in this exploration of the Roots of hip-hop and their prophetic calling, as well as the discernment of your calling, too. As I noted at the beginning of the book, this journey engaging the Roots is powerful as its own story. Yet it begs the question of each of our callings, and what we do with them. In the end, we all have to ponder, as Alexander Hamilton does, of "who does write our story." In one sense, of course, each of us authors our own story. One of the most interesting recent theological voices on vocation, Kathleen Cahalan, writes that one's calling "is inherently narrative" and its "first language is story."[20] However, it is not a straightforward thing to tell our stories—to others, and to ourselves. Cahalan argues the complexity of life today makes the task of making sense of one's life quite challenging. This is especially true given that, as she argues, callings unfold over a lifetime, and take on a more complex shape just as our lives and engagement with the world does the same. In another sense, and perhaps the more primal one, Cahalan writes, our stories and calling emerge not just from ourselves, but in response to the "One-Who-Calls." As the womanist theologian Emily Townes, drawing on Toni Morrison's novel *Beloved*, puts it,

> to be called beloved
> is to be called by God
> to be called by the shining moments
> to be called deep within deep
> to be called beloved
> is the marvelous yes to God's what if
> the radical shifting growth
> mundane agency of active faith.[21]

20. Cahalan and Miller-McLemore, *Calling All Years Good*, 6.
21. Townes, *In a Blaze of Glory*, 47.

Telling the story of the One-Who-Calls, the source of our sense of calling and also our guide to the shape of living it out, is essential to filling out the background of a prophetic calling that responds to the "cry" of suffering with actions rooted in love and justice.

The Roots (and many hip-hop artists) have signaled in their music and in interviews and writing that they draw on faith convictions and traditions.[22] For many people today, faith convictions are not easily held onto, especially in this age of splintered understandings of God and spirituality, and a fast-growing demographic not connected to any faith traditions whatsoever.[23] Yet as the United States moves through the spasms of transition from white majority to white minority, and faces a fierce reckoning over white supremacy and racial justice as it does, we could hardly ask for more trustworthy prophetic guides to the promise of this land called America. The authenticity of the Roots' calling—and their ways of living it out on one of the biggest platforms offered in our society—gives a credibility to such faith-rooted prophetic living that may inspire others. In writing this book, I especially hope to encourage people who, as Ta-Nehisi Coates puts it, "believe themselves to be white."[24] In humbly sitting at the feet of teachers like the Roots, white people may be formed in their own prophetic calling literally by "Black Thought," that is, in ways that are responsive to racial and social justice, especially concerning the plight of Black Americans.

The Roots *are* living their prophetic calling—having found their way through early years of play, to a passionate engagement in their art, and pairing this passion with

22. Hodge, *Baptized in Dirty Water*.
23. Taylor, *Secular Age*. Zuckerman, *Society Without God*.
24. Coates, *Between the World and Me*, 97.

a purpose—living their version of hip-hop as, Thompson calls it, "upstart Black folk music." They have never lost their joy in playing "good music" as their early track embodied. I love that the earlier stages of the development of one's calling do not go away, but persist as part of finding one's purpose. Play, to be specific, does not go away, but persists inside of passion, helping allow a fullness and maturity to living with purpose. Trotter describes something akin to this when he says:

> What I do on *The Tonight Show* helps me to sharpen my sword because I get a chance to interact with my band mates every day and I get to hone my musicianship and freestyle or improvise when need be. But more than those things, it's a chance for me to exercise some other muscles that I don't get to apply to my music as often, which is the side of humor. I get to be funny and I get to inject a certain amount of silliness and levity and lightheartedness that when I'm working in The Roots capacity isn't always necessarily the case. And even more certainly not the case when I'm working as a solo artist. I feel like there's a gravitas that is associated with my brand as an emcee and as a creative, and I try to remain mindful of that. But when I'm on *The Tonight Show*, I'm able to let my guard down and be vulnerable and be funny in a different way.[25]

Despite it all, the Roots are, like the prophets of old, both telling the hard truth of oppression and suffering, and casting visions of hope and joy. They embody the argument that arts—hip-hop included—are a vital medium for fulfilling that prophetic calling. It seems fitting to give the last word to the MC. Trotter puts it this way:

25. Uitti, "Black Thought Wants to Speak Truth to Power."

I feel like now more than ever there's space for everything to coexist. It's a beautiful time to be alive because of that. I feel like the filter has been completely taken off, and in many regards, the Band-Aid has been torn off. There's space for the real shit to be said and for the real stories to be told and the real pictures to be painted and the real photographs to be posted. So I think it's a dope time to be alive, and a beautiful time to be an artist.[26]

May it be so for you, too, dear reader, as you find and live a prophetic calling in the world.

---

26. Uitti, "Black Thought Wants to Speak Truth to Power."

Bibliography

Alexander, Michelle. *The New Jim Crow: Mass Incarceration in an Age of Colorblindness*. New York: New Press, 2010.

"Barack Obama citizenship conspiracy theories." https://en.wikipedia. org/wiki/Barack_Obama_citizenship_conspiracy_theories.

Bellah, Robert. *Religion in Human Evolution: From the Paleolithic to the Axial Age*. Cambridge: Harvard University Press, 2017.

Bellah, Robert, and Heather Horn. "Where Does Religion Come From?" *The Atlantic*, August 17, 2011. https://www.theatlantic. com/entertainment/archive/2011/08/where-does-religion-come-from/243723/.

Bialik, Carl. "Is the Conventional Wisdom Correct in Measuring Hip-Hop Audience?" *The Wall Street Journal*, May 5, 2005. http:// www.wsj.com/articles/SB111521814339424546.

Bilger, Burkhard. "The Rhythm in Everything: A Hip-hop Pioneer Reinvents Late-Night Music." *The New Yorker*, November 12, 2012. http://www.newyorker.com/magazine/2012/11/12/the-rhythm-in-everything.

Brown, Kali. "Black History Art: Romare Bearden." http://kalibrown. com/kalijournals/2016/2/4/black-history-art-romare-bearden.

Cahalan, Kathleen A., and Bonnie J. Miller-McLemore, eds. *Calling All Years Good: Christian Vocation throughout Live's Seasons*. Grand Rapids: Eerdmans, 2017.

Chafin, Chris. "A Man of Many Names: A Lazy Afternoon with Questlove." *Brooklyn Magazine*, June 1, 2015. http://www.bkmag. com/2015/06/01/a-man-of-many-names-a-lazy-afternoon-with-questlove/.

Chang, Jeff. *Can't Stop, Won't Stop: A History of the Hip-Hop Generation*. New York: Picador, 2005.

———. "How Hip-Hop Got Its Name: The Origins of the Phrase Go Deeper than Sugarhill Gang." *Cuepoint*, October 10, 2014. https://medium.com/cuepoint/how-hip-hop-got-its-name-a3529fa4fbf1#.chr9uvau9.

Chinen, Nate. "How The Soulquarians Birthed D'Angelo's 'Voodoo' and Transformed Jazz." *The New York Times*, August 8, 2018. https://www.nytimes.com/2018/08/08/arts/music/playing-changes-excerpt-soulquarians-dangelo.html.

———. *Playing Changes: Jazz for the New Century*. New York: Pantheon, 2018.

Chion, Michel. "Requiem." https://www.subrosa.net/en/catalogue/early-electronic-music/michel-chion.html.

Coates, Ta-Nehisi. *Between the World and Me*. New York: Spiegel and Grau, 2015.

Cohn, Nate, and Kevin Quealy. "How Public Opinion has moved on Black Lives Matter." *The New York Times*, June 10, 2020. https://www.nytimes.com/interactive/2020/06/10/upshot/black-lives-matter-attitudes.html.

Cone, James. *The Cross and the Lynching Tree*. Maryknoll, NY: Orbis, 2011.

———. *The Spirituals and The Blues: An Interpretation*. Maryknoll, NY: Maryknoll, 1992.

Drake. "Started from the Bottom." https://www.youtube.com/watch?v=RubBzkZzpUA.

Dryden, Richard. "'Treats.' Art Director Kenny Gravillis Tells the Stories Behind The Roots' 5 'Things Fall Apart' Album Covers." https://www.complex.com/style/2014/02/the-roots-things-fall-apart-album-covers/woman-running.

Dunbar-Ortiz, Roxanne. *An Indigenous Peoples' History of the United States*. Boston: Beacon, 2014.

Fallon, Jimmy. "Questlove Remembers When Jimmy Won The Roots Over." *The Tonight Show*, May 3, 2016. https://www.youtube.com/watch?v=Vq3xDorarc8.

Gafney, Wilda. *Daughters of Miriam: Women Prophets in Ancient Israel*. Minneapolis: Fortress, 2008.

———. *Womanist Midrash: A Reintroduction toe the Women of the Torah and the Throne*. Louisville: Westminster John Knox, 2017.

Garrison, Lucas. "The Roots' ' . . . And Then You Shoot Your Cousin' Album Made Me A Better Music Fan." https://djbooth.net/features/roots-cousin-fan.

Gilbert, Kenyatta R. *A Pursued Justice: Black Preaching from the Great Migration to Civil Rights.* Waco, TX: Baylor University Press, 2016.

Gross, Terri. "Questlove's Roots." Interview on NPR's Fresh Air broadcast, June 24, 2013. http://www.npr.org/2013/06/24/190420270/questloves-roots-a-meta-memoir-of-a-lifetime-in-music.

Ghansah, Rachel Kaadzi. "Don't Let The Green Grass Fool You." *Politico,* December 14, 2011. http://www.politico.com/states/new-york/city-hall/story/2011/12/dont-let-the-green-grass-fool-you-the-roots-are-one-of-the-most-respected-hip-hop-acts-in-the-world-why-cant-they-leave-the-sad-stuff-alone-067223.

Goto, Courtney T. *The Grace of Playing: Pedagogies for Leaning Into God's New Creation.* Eugene, OR: Pickwick, 2016.

Hager, Steven. "Afrika Bambaataa's Hip-Hop." *The Village Voice,* September 1982.

Hodge, Daniel White. *Baptized in Dirty Water: Reimagining the Gospel according to Tupac Amaru Shakur.* Eugene, OR: Cascade, 2019.

———. *Heaven has a Ghetto.* Verlag, 2010.

Iyer, Vijay. *Memorophilia.* Asian Improv Records 1995, liner notes.

———. Personal conversation. Colorado College Artist Series. Colorado Springs, CO. May 9, 2019.

Jennings, Willie James. *The Christian Imagination: A Theology and the Origins of Race.* New Haven, CT: Yale University Press, 2010.

Jobe, Sarah. "Reading Jael's story in a women's prison: What does Judges 4–5 mean to abused women who fought back?" *The Christian Century,* October 10, 2018. https://www.christiancentury.org/article/critical-essay/reading-jael-s-story-women-s-prison.

Jones, Robert P. "Self-Segregation: Why It's So Hard for Whites to Understand Ferguson." *The Atlantic,* August 21, 2014. https://www.theatlantic.com/national/archive/2014/08/self-segregation-why-its-hard-for-whites-to-understand-ferguson/378928/.

Junior, Nyasha. *An Introduction to Womanist Biblical Interpretation.* Louisville: Westminster/John Knox, 2015.

Leas, Ryan. "We've Got A File On You: Black Thought." https://www.stereogum.com/2102263/black-thought-roots-end-game-solo-albums-chadwick-boseman-kanye-west/franchises/interview/weve-got-a-file-on-you/.

Lee, Spike. *Mo' Better Blues.* 40 Acres and a Mule Productions, August 3, 1990.

Madden, Michael. "The Roots—. . . And Then You Shoot Your Cousin." https://consequenceofsound.net/2014/05/album-review-the -roots-and-then-you-shoot-your-cousin/?utm_expid=.I2Ok ZS06Riahk3UovrA5rQ.o&utm_referrer=https%3A%2F% 2Fwww.google.com%2F.

Mason, Anthony. "The Roots of Questlove's Success." *CBS News,* September 14, 2014. http://www.cbsnews.com/news/the-roots-of-questloves-success/.

Metropolis Ensemble. "The Roots' And Then You Shoot Your Cousin." https://metropolisensemble.org/albums/the-roots-and-then-you-shoot-your-cousin.

Moon, Tom. "The Roots: A Song Cycle for a Life Cycle." *NPR,* December 6, 2011. http://www.npr.org/2011/12/06/143203876/ the-roots-a-song-cycle-for-a-life-cycle.

NPR Staff. "The Roots Weave a Tale of Crime and Karma." *NPR,* December 18, 2011. http://www.npr.org/2011/12 /18/143891292/the-roots-weave-a-tale-of-crime-and-karma, accessed August 25, 2016.

———. "The Roots: Rising Up with Rising Down." *NPR,* April 28, 2008. https://www.npr.org/templates/story/story. php?storyId=90025197.

O'Donohue, John. *Anam Cara: A Book of Celtic Wisdom.* New York: HarperCollins, 1998.

Padilla, Elaine. *Divine Enjoyment: A Theology of Passion and Exuberance.* New York: Fordham University Press, 2015.

Parham, Marisa. "You Can't Flow Over This: Ursula Rucker's Acoustic Illusion." In *Sonic Interventions,* edited by Sylvia Mieszkowski et al., 87–100. New York: Rodopi, 2008.

Phillips, Yoh. "What Better Hip-Hop? Be A Better Fan." https:// djbooth.net/features/be-a-better-fan.

Powers, Stephen. The Roots Freestyle video. https://www.youtube. com/watch?v=t4xrTaAOLHQ.

Reeves, Mosi. "The Roots' Black Thought on How He Spit a Nearly 10-Minute Viral Freestyle." *Rolling Stone,* December 26, 2017. https://www.rollingstone.com/music/music-features/the-roots-black-thought-on-how-he-spit-nearly-10-minute-viral-freestyle-197206/.

Roots, The. "The Roots x A-Trak—"Never" f. Patty Crash Live on The Tonight Show." https://www.dailymotion.com/video/x1vxkgb.

———. "The Roots—Star." https://www.youtube.com/watch?v=8Z9 HvjbAYtA.

Rucker, Ursula. "Ursula Rucker." Interviewed by Stephan Oettel. https://www.irieites.de/interviews/Ursula%20Rucker_Interview. htm.

Rys, Dan. "The Roots Black Thought on Lin-Manuel Miranda." https://www.billboard.com/articles/columns/hip-hop/7595776/ hamilton-mixtape-the-roots-black-thought-on-lin-manuel-miranda.

———. "The Roots' New Project will be a Concept Album." https:// www.xxlmag.com/the-roots-new-project-will-be-another-concept-album/?utm_source=tsmclip&utm_medium=referral.

Rytlewski, Evan. "The Roots lay on the satire with the arty . . . *And Then You Shoot Your Cousin.*" https://music.avclub.com/the-roots-lay-on-the-satire-with-the-arty-and-then-you-1798180522.

Scaggs, Austin. "The Roots of the Roots." *Rolling Stone,* May 15, 2008. https://www.rollingstone.com/music/music-news/the-roots-of-the-roots-242428/.

Scharen, Christian. *Broken Hallelujahs: Why Popular Music Matters to Those Seeking God.* Grand Rapids: Brazos, 2011.

———. "Eclipsing: The Loss and Recovery of Practical Wisdom in the Modern West." In *Christian Practical Wisdom: What it is, Why it Matters,* edited by Dorothy Bass et. al., 145–74 Grand Rapids: Eerdmans, 2016.

Schulte, Tom. "Review of Michael Chion, Requiem." https://www.all-music.com/album/requiem-mw0000752889.

Schwartz, Mattathias. "Street Art and Subversion from Stephen (ESPO) Powers." *The New Yorker,* November 24, 2015. https:// www.newyorker.com/culture/culture-desk/street-art-and-subversion-from-stephen-espo-powers.

Serrano, Shea. *The Rap Year Book: The Most Important Rap Songs from Every Year Since 1979, Discussed, Debated, and Deconstructed.* New York: Abrams Image, 2015.

Taylor, Charles. *A Secular Age.* Cambridge, MA: Harvard University Press, 2006.

Thompson, Ahmir "Questlove." Interview on Fuse. https://www.you-tube.com/watch?v=QUHVgnLuw14.

——— "The Roots: Getting Personal in 'How I Got Over.'" *NPR,* June 25, 2010. http://www.npr.org/2010/06/25/127911510/the-roots-getting-personal-in-how-i-got-over.d.

———. "Questlove (2013)." http://www.redbullmusicacademy.com/ lectures/questlove-new-york-2013.

———. "Questlove: Does Black Culture Need to Care About What Happens to Hip-Hop?" *Vulture,* May 27, 2014. http://www.

vulture.com/2014/05/questlove-part-6-does-black-culture-need-to-care-about-hip-hop.html.

———. "Questlove on 'Hamilton' and Hip-Hop: It Takes One." *Rolling Stone*, September 28, 2015. https://www.rollingstone.com/culture/culture-news/questlove-on-hamilton-and-hip-hop-it-takes-one-34370/.

———. "When the People Cheer: How Hip Hop Failed Black America." *Vulture*, April 22, 2014. https://www.vulture.com/2014/04/questlove-on-how-hip-hop-failed-black-america.html.

Thompson, Ahmir "Questlove," and Ben Greenman. *Mo' Meta Blues: The World According to Questlove*. New York: Hachette, 2013.

Trotter, Tariq. Freestyle at HOT 97 with Funk Flex. https://www.youtube.com/watch?v=prmQgSpV3fA.

Townes, Emilie. *In a Blaze of Glory: Womanist Spirituality as Social Witness*. Nashville: Abingdon, 1995.

———. "Womanist Theology." In *Encyclopedia of Women and Religion in North America*, edited by Rosemary Skinner Keller and Rosemary Radford Ruether, 1165–72. Bloomington: Indiana University Press, 2006.

Uitti, Jacob. "Black Thought Wants to Speak Truth to Power." https://www.interviewmagazine.com/music/black-thought-the-roots-truth-power.

Wagner, Tony. *Creating Innovators: The Making of Young People Who Will Change the World*. New York: Scribner, 2012.

Zuckerman, Phil. *Society Without God: What the Least Religious Nations Can Tell Us About Contentment*. New York: New York University Press, 2008.